YEARS OF MY YOUTH

BY

WILLIAM DEAN HOWELLS

BOOKS FOR LIBRARIES PRESS
FREEPORT, NEW YORK

INTERNATIONAL STANDARD BOOK NUMBER:
0-8369-5626-5

LIBRARY OF CONGRESS CATALOG CARD NUMBER:
70-146859

PRINTED IN THE UNITED STATES OF AMERICA

YEARS OF MY YOUTH

YEARS OF MY YOUTH

I

IT is hard to know the child's own earliest recollections from the things it has been told of itself by those with whom its life began. They remember for it the past which it afterward seems to remember for itself; the wavering outline of its nature is shadowed against the background of family, and from this it imagines an individual existence which has not yet begun. The events then have the quality of things dreamt, not lived, and they remain of that impalpable and elusive quality in all the after years.

I

Of the facts which I must believe from the witness of others, is the fact that I was born on the 1st of March, 1837, at Martin's Ferry, Belmont County, Ohio. My father's name was William Cooper Howells, and my mother's was Mary Dean; they were married six years before my birth, and I was the second child in their family of eight. On my father's side my people were wholly Welsh, except his English grandmother, and on my mother's side wholly German, except her Irish father, of whom it is mainly known that he knew how to win my grandmother Elizabeth Dock away from her very loving family, where they dwelt in great Pennsylvania-German comfort and prosperity on their farm near Harrisburg, to share with him the hardships of the wild country over the westward mountains. She was the favorite of her brothers and sisters, and the best-beloved of her mother, perhaps because she was the youngest; there is a shadowy legend that she went one evening to milk the cows, and did not return from following after her husband; but I cannot associate this romantic story with the ageing grandmother whom I tenderly loved when a child, and whom I still fondly remember. She spoke with a strong German accent, and she had her Luther Bible, for she never read English. Sometimes she came to visit my homesick mother after we went to live in southern Ohio; once I went with my mother to visit her in the little town where I was born, and of that visit I have the remembrance of her stopping me on the stairs, one morning when I had been out, and asking me in her German idiom and accent, "What fur a tay is it, child?"

I can reasonably suppose that it is because of the mixture of Welsh, German, and Irish in me that I feel myself so typically American, and that I am of the imaginative temperament which has enabled me all the conscious years of my life to see reality more iridiscent and beautiful, or more lurid and terrible than any make-believe about reality. Among my father's people the first who left Wales was his great-grandfather. He established himself in London as a clock and watch maker, and I like to believe that it is his name which my tall clock, paneled in the lovely *chinoiserie* of Queen Anne's time, bears graven on its dial. Two sons followed him, and wrought at the same art, then almost a fine art, and one of them married in London and took his English wife back with him to Wales. His people were, so far as my actual knowledge goes, middle-class Welsh, but the family is of such a remote antiquity as in its present dotage not to know what part

4

of Wales it came from. As to our lineage a Welsh clergy-man, a few years ago, noting the identity of name, in-vited me to the fond conjecture of descent from Hywel Dda, or Howel the Good, who became king of Wales about the time of Alfred the Great. He codified the laws or rather the customs of his realm, and produced one of the most interesting books I have read, and I have finally preferred him as an ancestor because he was the first literary man of our name. There was a time when I leaned toward the delightful James Howell, who wrote the *Familiar Letters* and many books in verse and prose, and was of several shades of politics in the difficult days of Charles and Oliver; but I was forced to relinquish him be-cause he was never married. My father, for his part, when once questioned as to our origin, answered that so far as he could make out we derived from a blacksmith, whom he considered a good sort of ancestor, but he could not name him, and he must have been, whatever his merit, a person of extreme obscurity.

There is no record of the time when my great-grand-father with his brothers went to London and fixed there as watchmakers. My tall clock, which bears our name on its dial, has no date, and I can only imagine their London epoch to have begun about the middle of the eighteenth century. Being Welsh, they were no doubt musical, and I like to cherish the tradition of singing and playing women in our line, and a somehow cousinship with the famous Parepa. But this is very uncertain; what is certain is that when my great-grandfather went back to Wales he fixed himself in the little town of Hay, where he began the manufacture of Welsh flannels, a fabric still esteemed for its many virtues, and greatly prospered. When I visited Hay in 1883 (my father always call it, after the old fashion, The Hay, which was the right version of its Norman name of La

Haye), three of his mills were yet standing, and one of them was working, very modestly, on the sloping bank of the lovely river Wye. Another had sunk to be a stable, but the third, in the spirit of our New World lives, had become a bookstore and printing-office, a well-preserved stone edifice of four or five stories, such as there was not the like of, probably, in the whole of Wales when Hywel Dda was king. My great-grandfather was apparently an excellent business man, but I am afraid I must own (reluctantly, with my Celtic prejudice) that literature, or the love of it, came into our family with the English girl whom he married in London. She was, at least, a reader of the fiction of the day, if I may judge from the high-colored style of the now pathetically faded letter which she wrote to reproach a daughter who had made a runaway match and fled to America. So many people then used to make runaway matches; but when very late in the lives of these eloping lovers I once saw them, an old man and woman, at our house in Columbus, they hardly looked their youthful adventure, even to the fancy of a boy beginning to unrealize life. The reader may care to learn that they were the ancestors of Vaughan Kester, the very gifted young novelist, who came into popular recognition almost in the hour of his most untimely death, and of his brother Paul Kester, the playwright.

II

My great-grandfather became "a Friend by Convincement," as the Quakers called the Friends not born in their Society; but I do not know whether it was before or after his convincement that he sailed to Philadelphia with a stock of his Welsh flannels, which he sold to such advantage that a dramatic family tradition represents him wheeling the proceeds in a barrel of silver down the street to the vessel which brought him and which took him away. That was in the time of Washington's second Presidency, and Washington strongly advised his staying in the country and setting up his manufacture here; but he was prospering in Wales, and why should he come to America even at the suggestion of Washington? It is another family tradition that he complied so far as to purchase a vast acreage of land on the Potomac, including the site of our present capital, as some of his descendants in each generation have believed, without the means of expropriating the nation from its unlawful holdings. This would have been the more difficult as he never took a deed of his land, and he certainly never came back to America; yet he seems always to have been haunted by the allurement of it which my grandfather felt so potently that after twice visiting the country he came over a third time and cast his lot here.

He was already married, when with his young wife and my father a year old he sailed from London in 1808. Perhaps because they were chased by a French privateer, they speedily arrived in Boston after a voyage of only twenty-one days. In the memoir which my father wrote for his family, and which was published after his death, he tells that my grandmother formed the highest opinion of Boston, mainly, he surmises, from the very intelligent behavior of the young ladies in making a pet of her baby at the boarding-house where she stayed while her husband began going about wherever people wished his skill in setting up woolen-mills. The young ladies taught her little one to walk; and many years afterward, say fifty, when I saw her for the last time in a village of northwestern Ohio, she said "the Bostonians were very nice people," so faithfully had she cherished, through a thousand vicissitudes, the kind memory of that first sojourn in America.

I do not think she quite realized the pitch of greatness at which I had arrived in writing for the *Atlantic Monthly*, the renowned periodical then recently founded in Boston, or the fame of the poets whom I had met there the year before. I suspect that she was never of the literary taste of my English great-grandmother; but her father had been a school-teacher, and she had been carefully educated by the uncle and aunt to whom she was left at her parents' early death. They were Friends, but she never formally joined the Society, though worshiping with them; she was, like her husband, middle-class Welsh, and as long as they lived they both misplaced their aspirates. If I add that her maiden name was Thomas, and that her father's name was John Thomas, I think I have sufficiently attested her pure Cymric origin. So far as I know there was no mixture of Saxon blood on her side; but her people, like most of the border Welsh, spoke the languages of both races; and very late in my father's life, he mentioned casually, as old people will mention interesting things, that he remembered his father and mother speaking Welsh together. Of the two she remained the fonder of their native country, and in that last visit I paid her she said, after half a century of exile, "We do so and so at home, and you do so and so here." I can see her now, the gentlest of little Quaker ladies, with her white fichu crossed on her breast; and I hesitate attributing to her my immemorial knowledge that the Welsh were never conquered, but were tricked into union with the English by having one of their princes born, as it were surreptitiously, in Wales; it must have been my father who told me this and amused himself with my childish race-pride in the fact. She gave me an illustrated *Tour of Wales*, having among its steel-engravings the picture of a Norman castle where, by favor of a cousin who was the housekeeper, she had slept one night when a girl; but in America she had slept oftener in log cabins, which my grandfather satisfied his devoted unworldliness in making his earthly tabernacles. She herself was not, I think, a devout person; she had her spiritual life in his, and followed his varying fortunes, from richer to poorer, with a tacit adherence to what he believed, whether the mild doctrine of Quakerism or the fervid Methodism for which he never quite relinquished it.

He seems to have come to America with money enough to lose a good deal in his removals from Boston to Poughkeepsie, from Poughkeepsie to New York City, from New York to Virginia, and from Virginia to eastern Ohio, where he ended in such adversity on his farm that he was glad to accept the charge of a woolen-mill in Steubenville. He knew the business thoroughly and he had set up mills for others in his various sojourns, following the line of least resistance among the Quaker settlements opened to him by the letters he had brought from Wales. He even went to the new capital, Washington, in a hope of manufacturing in Virginia held out to him by a nephew of President Madison, but it failed him to his heavy cost; and in Ohio, his farming experiments, which he renewed in a few years on giving up that mill at Steubenville, were alike disastrous. After more than enough of them he rested for a while in Wheeling, West Virginia, where my father met my mother, and they were married.

They then continued the family wanderings in his own search for the chance of earning a living in what seems to have been a very grudging country, even to industry so willing as his. He had now become a printer, and not that only, but a publisher, for he had already begun and ended the issue of a monthly magazine called *The Gleaner*, made up, as its name implied, chiefly of selections; his

9

sister helped him as editor, and some old bound volumes of its few numbers show their joint work to have been done with good taste in the preferences of their day. He married upon the expectation of affluence from the publication of a work on *The Rise, Progress and Downfall of Aristocracy*, which almost immediately preceded the ruin of the enthusiastic author and of my father with him, if he indeed could have experienced further loss in his entire want of money. He did not lose heart, and he was presently living contentedly on three hundred dollars a year as foreman of a newspaper office in St. Clairville, Ohio. But his health gave way, and a little later, for the sake of the outdoor employment, he took up the trade of house-painter; and he was working at this in Wheeling when my grandfather Dean suggested his buying a lot and building a house in Martin's Ferry, just across the Ohio River. The lot must have been bought on credit, and he built mainly with his own capable hands a small brick house of one story and two rooms with a lean-to. In this house I was born, and my father and mother were very happy there; they never owned another house until their children helped them work and pay for it a quarter of a century afterward, though throughout this long time they made us a home inexpressibly dear to me still.

My father now began to read medicine, but during the course of a winter's lectures at Cincinnati (where he worked as a printer meanwhile), his health again gave way and he returned to Martin's Ferry. When I was three years old, my grandmother Dean's eldest brother, William Dock, came to visit her. He was the beloved patriarch of a family which I am glad to claim my kindred and was a best type of his Pennsylvania-German race. He had prospered on through a life of kindness and good deeds; he was so rich that he had driven in his own car-

YEARS OF MY YOUTH

riage from Harrisburg, over the mountains, and he now asked my father to drive with him across the state of Ohio. When they arrived in Dayton, my father went on by canal to Hamilton, where he found friends to help him buy the Whig newspaper which he had only just paid for when he sold it eight years later.

Of the first three years of my life which preceded this removal there is very little that I can honestly claim to remember. The things that I seem to remember are seeing from the window of our little house, when I woke one morning, a peach-tree in bloom; and again seeing from the steamboat which was carrying our family to Cincinnati, a man drowning in the river. But these visions, both of them very distinct, might very well have been the effect of hearing the things spoken of by my elders, though I am surest of the peach-tree in bloom as an authentic memory.

This time, so happy for my father and mother, was scarcely less happy because of its uncertainties. My young aunts lived with their now widowed mother not far from us; as the latest comer, I was in much request among them, of course; and my father was hardly less in favor with the whole family from his acceptable habit of finding a joke in everything. He supplied the place of son to my grandmother in the absence of my young uncles, then away most of their time on the river which they followed from the humblest beginnings on keel-boats to the proudest endings as pilots and captains and owners of steamboats. In those early days when they returned from the river they brought their earnings to their mother in gold coins, which they called Yellow Boys, and which she kept in a bowl in the cupboard, where I

11

seem so vividly to have seen them, that I cannot quite believe I did not. These good sons were all Democrats except the youngest, but they finally became of my father's anti-slavery Whig faith in politics, and I believe they were as glad to have their home in a free state as my father's family, who had now left Wheeling, and were settled in southwestern Ohio.

There were not many slaves in Wheeling, but it was a sort of entrepôt where the negroes were collected and embarked for the plantations down the river, in their doom to the death-in-life of the far South. My grand-father Howells had, in the anti-slavery tradition of his motherland, made himself so little desired among his Virginian fellow-citizens that I have heard his removal from Wheeling was distinctly favored by public sentiment; and afterward, on the farm he bought in Ohio, his fences and corn-cribs suffered from the pro-slavery convictions of his neighbors. But he was dwelling in safety and prosperity among the drugs and books which were his merchandise in the store where I began to remember him in my earliest days at Hamilton. He seemed to me a very old man, and I noticed with the keen observance of a child how the muscles sagged at the sides of his chin and how his under lip, which I did not know I had inherited from him, projected. His clothes, which had long ceased to be drab in color, were of a Quaker formality in cut; his black hat followed this world's fashion in color, but was broad in the brim and very low-crowned, which added somehow in my young sense to the reproving sadness of his presence. He had black Welsh eyes and was of the low stature of his race; my grandmother was blue-eyed; she was little, too; but my aunt, their only surviving daughter, with his black eyes, was among their taller children. She was born several years after their settlement in America, but she loyally misused her aspirates as they did, and, never marrying, was of a life-long devotion to them. They first lived over the drug-store, after the fashion of shopkeepers in England; I am aware of my grandfather soon afterward having a pretty house and a large garden quite away from the store, but he always lived more simply than his means obliged. Amidst the rude experiences of their backwoods years, the family had continued gentle in their thoughts and tastes, though my grandfather shared with poetry his passion for religion, and in my later boyhood when I had begun to print my verses, he wrote me a letter solemnly praising them, but adjuring me to devote my gifts to the service of my Maker, which I had so little notion of doing in a selfish ideal of my own glory.

Most of his father's fortune had somehow gone to other sons, but, whether rich or poor, their generation seemed to be of a like religiosity. One of them lived in worldly state at Bristol before coming to America, and was probably of a piety not so insupportable as I found him in the memoir which he wrote of his second wife, when I came to read it the other day. Him I never saw, but from time to time there was one or other of his many sons employed in my grandfather's store, whom I remember blithe spirits, disposed to seize whatever chance of a joke life offered them, such as selling Young's *Night Thoughts* to a customer who had whispered his wish for an improper book. Some of my father's younger brothers were of a like cheerfulness with these lively cousins, and of the same aptness for laughter. One was a physician, another a dentist, another in a neighboring town a druggist, another yet a speculative adventurer in the regions to the southward: he came back from his commercial forays once with so many half-dollars that when spread out they covered the whole surface of our dining-table; but I am quite unable to report what negotiation they were the spoil of. There was a far cousin who was a painter, and left (possibly as a pledge of indebtedness) with my dentist uncle after a sojourn among us a picture which I early prized as a masterpiece, and still remember as the charming head of a girl shadowed by the fan she held over it. I never saw the painter, but I recall, from my father's singing them, the lines of a "doleful ballad" which he left behind him as well as the picture:

A thief will steal from you all that you havye,
But an unfaithful lovyer will bring you to your grave.

The uncle who was a physician, when he left off the practice of medicine about his eightieth year, took up the art of sculpture; he may have always had a taste for it, and his knowledge of anatomy would have helped qualify him for it. He modeled from photographs a head of my father admirably like and full of character, the really extraordinary witness of a gift latent till then through a long life devoted to other things.

We children had our preference among these Howells uncles, but we did not care for any of them so much as for our Dean uncles, who now and then found their way up to Hamilton from Cincinnati when their steamboats lay there in their trips from Pittsburg. They were all very jovial; and one of the younger among them could play the violin, not less acceptably because he played by ear and not by art. Of the youngest and best-loved I am lastingly aware in his coming late one night and of my creeping down-stairs from my sleep to sit in his lap and hear his talk with my father and mother, while his bursts of laughter agreeably shook my small person. I dare say these uncles used to bring us gifts from that steamboating world of theirs which seemed to us of a splendor not less than what I should now call oriental when we sometimes visited them at Cincinnati, and came away bulging in every pocket with the more portable of the dainties we had been feasting upon. In the most signal of these visits, as I once sat between my father and my Uncle William, for whom I was named, on the hurricane roof of his boat, he took a silver half-dollar from his pocket and put it warm in my hand, with a quizzical look into my eyes. The sight of such unexampled riches stopped my breath for the moment, but I made out to ask, "Is it for me?" and he nodded his head smilingly up and down; then, for my experience had hitherto been of fippenny-bits yielded by my father after long reasoning, I asked, "Is it good?" and remained puzzled to know why they laughed so together; it must have been years before I understood.

These uncles had grown up in a slave state, and they thought, without thinking, that slavery must be right; but once when an abolition lecturer was denied public hearing at Martin's Ferry, they said he should speak in their mother's house; and there, much unaware, I heard my first and last abolition lecture, barely escaping with my life, for one of the objections urged by the mob outside was a stone hurled through the window, where my mother sat with me in her arms. At my Uncle William's house in the years after the Civil War, my father and he began talking of old times, and he told how, when a boy on a keel-boat, tied up to a Mississippi shore, he had seen an overseer steal upon a black girl loitering at her work, and wind his blacksnake-whip round her body, naked except for the one cotton garment she wore. "When I heard that colored female screech," he said, and the old-fashioned word female, used for compassionate respectfulness, remains with me, "and saw her jump, I knew that there must be something wrong in slavery." Perhaps the sense of this had been in his mind when he

15

YEARS OF MY YOUTH

determined with his brothers that the abolition lecturer
should be heard in their mother's house.

She sometimes came to visit us in Hamilton, to break
the homesick separations from her which my mother suffered through for so many years, and her visits were times
of high holiday for us children. I should be interested
now to know what she and my Welsh grandmother made
of each other, but I believe they were good friends,
though probably not mutually very intelligible. My
mother's young sisters, who also came on welcome visits,
were always joking with my father and helping my mother
at her work; but I cannot suppose that there was much
common ground between them and my grandfather's
family except in their common Methodism. For me, I
adored them; and if the truth must be told, though I
had every reason to love my Welsh grandmother, I had a
peculiar tenderness for my Pennsylvania-Dutch grandmother, with her German accent and her caressing ways.
My grandfather, indeed, could have recognized no difference among heirs of equal complicity in Adam's sin;
and in the situation such as it was, I lived blissfully un-
born to all things of life outside of my home. I can recur
to the time only as a dream of love and loving, and though
I came out of it no longer a little child, but a boy struggling tooth and nail for my place among other boys, I must
still recur to the ten or eleven years passed in Hamilton
as the gladdest of all my years. They may have been
even gladder than they now seem, because the incidents
which embody happiness had then the novelty which
such incidents lose from their recurrence; while the
facts of unhappiness, no matter how often they repeat
themselves, seem throughout life an unprecedented experience and impress themselves as vividly the last time as the
first. I recall some occasions of grief and shame in that
far past with unfailing distinctness, but the long spaces

16

of blissful living which they interrupted hold few or no records which I can allege in proof of my belief that I was then, above every other when,

Joyful and free from blame.

IV

Throughout those years at Hamilton I think of my father as absorbed in the mechanical and intellectual work of his newspaper. My earliest sense of him relates him as much to the types and the press as to the table where he wrote his editorials amidst the talk of the printers, or of the politicians who came to discuss public affairs with him. From a quaint pride, he did not like his printer's craft to be called a trade; he contended that it was a profession; he was interested in it, as the expression of his taste, and the exercise of his ingenuity and invention, and he could supply many deficiencies in its means and processes. He cut fonts of large type for job-work out of apple-wood in default of box or olive; he even made the graver's tools for carving the letters. Nothing pleased him better than to contrive a thing out of something it was not meant for, as making a penknife blade out of an old razor, or the like. He could do almost anything with his ready hand and his ingenious brain, while I have never been able to do anything with mine but write a few score books. But as for the printer's craft with me, it was simply my joy and pride from the first things I knew of it. I know when I could not read, for I recall supplying the text from my imagination for the pictures I found in books, but I do not know when I could not set type. My first attempt at literature was not written, but put up in type, and printed off by me. My father praised it, and this made me so proud that I showed

17

it to one of those eminent Whig politicians always haunting the office. He made no comment on it, but asked me if I could spell baker. I spelled the word simple-heartedly, and it was years before I realized that he meant a hurt to my poor little childish vanity.

Very soon I could set type very well, and at ten years and onward till journalism became my university, the printing-office was mainly my school. Of course, like every sort of work with a boy, the work became irksome to me, and I would gladly have escaped from it to every sort of play, but it never ceased to have the charm it first had. Every part of the trade became familiar to me, and if I had not been so little I could at once have worked not only at case, but at press, as my brother did. I had my favorites among the printers, who knew me as the Old Man, because of the habitual gravity which was apt to be broken in me by bursts of wild hilarity; but I am not sure whether I liked better the conscience of the young journeyman who wished to hold me in the leash of his moral convictions, or the nature of my companion in laughter which seemed to have selected for him the fit name of Sim Haggett. This merrymaker was married, but so very presently in our acquaintance was widowed, that I can scarcely put any space between his mourning for his loss and his rejoicing in the first joke that followed it. There were three or four of the journeymen, with an apprentice, to do the work now reduced by many facilities to the competence of one or two. Some of them slept in a den opening from the printing-office, where I envied them the wild freedom unhampered by the conventions of sweeping, dusting, or bed-making; it was next to camping out.

The range of that young experience of mine transcends telling, but the bizarre mixture was pure delight to the boy I was, already beginning to take the impress of events and characters. Though I loved the art of printing so much, though my pride even more than my love was taken with it, as something beyond other boys, yet I loved my schools too. In their succession there seem to have been a good many of them, with a variety of teachers, whom I tried to make like me because I liked them. I was gifted in spelling, geography, and reading, but arithmetic was not for me. I could declaim long passages from the speeches of Corwin against the Mexican War, and of Chatham against the American War, and poems from our school readers, or from Campbell or Moore or Byron; but at the blackboard I was dumb. I bore fairly well the mockeries of boys, boldly bad, who played upon a certain simplicity of soul in me, and pretended, for instance, when I came out one night saying I was six years old, that I was a shameless boaster and liar. Swimming, hunting, fishing, foraging at every season, with the skating which the waters of the rivers and canals afforded, were my joy; I took my part in the races and the games, in football and in baseball, then in its feline infancy of Three Corner Cat, and though there was a family rule against fighting, I fought like the rest of the boys and took my defeats as heroically as I knew how; they were mostly defeats.

My world was full of boys, but it was also much haunted by ghosts or the fear of them. Death came early into it, the visible image in a negro babe, with the large red copper cents on its eyelids, which older boys brought me to see, then in the funeral of the dearly loved mate whom we school-fellows followed to his grave. I learned many things in my irregular schooling, and at home I was always reading when I was not playing. I will not pretend that I did not love playing best; life was an experiment which had to be tried in every way that presented itself, but outside of these practical requisitions there was a constant demand upon me from literature. As to the playing I will not speak at large here, for I have already said enough of it in *A Boy's Town;* and as to the reading, the curious must go for it to another book of mine called *My Literary Passions.* Perhaps there was already in my early literary preferences a bent toward the reality which my gift, if I may call it so, has since taken. I did not willingly read poetry, except such pieces as I memorized: little tragedies of the sad fate of orphan children, and the cruelties of large birds to small ones, which brought the lump into my throat, or the moralized song of didactic English writers of the eighteenth century, such as "Pity the sorrows of a poor old man." That piece I still partly know by heart; but history was what I liked best, and if I finally turned to fiction it seems to have been in the dearth of histories that merited reading after Goldsmith's Greece and Rome; except Irving's *Conquest of Granada,* I found none that I could read; but I had then read *Don Quixote* and *Gulliver's Travels,* and had heard my father reading aloud to my mother the poems of Scott and Moore. Since he seems not to have thought of any histories that would meet my taste, I fancy that I must have been mainly left to my own choice in that sort, though he told me of the other sorts of books which I read.

I should be interested to know now how the notion of authorship first crept into my mind, but I do not in the least know. I made verses, I even wrote plays in rhyme, but until I attempted an historical romance I had no sense of literature as an art. As an art which one might live by, as by a trade or a business, I had not the slightest conception of it. When I began my first and last historical romance, I did not imagine it as something to be read by others; and when the first chapters were shown without my knowing, I was angry and ashamed. If my father thought there was anything uncommon in my small performances, he did nothing to let me guess it unless I must count the instance of declaiming Hallock's *Marco Bozzaris* before a Swedenborgian minister who was passing the night at our house. Neither did my mother do anything to make me conscious, if she was herself conscious of anything out of the common in what I was trying. It was her sacred instinct to show no partiality among her children; my father's notion was of the use that could be combined with the pleasure of life, and perhaps if there had been anything different in my life, it would not have tended more to that union of use and pleasure which was his ideal.

Much in the environment was abhorrent to him, and he fought the local iniquities in his paper, the gambling, the drunkenness that marred the mainly moral and religious complexion of the place. In *A Boy's Town* I have studied with a fidelity which I could not emulate here the whole life of it as a boy sees life, and I must leave the reader who cares for such detail to find it there. But I wish again to declare the almost unrivaled fitness of the place to be the home of a boy, with its two branches of the Great Miami River and their freshets in spring, and their witchery at all seasons; with its Hydraulic Channels and Reservoirs, its stretch of the Miami Canal and the Canal Basin so fit for swimming in summer and skating in winter. The mills and factories which harnessed the Hydraulic to their industries were of resistless allure for the boys who frequented them when they could pass the guard of "No Admittance" on their doors, or when they were not foraging among the fields and woods in the endless vacations of the schools. Some boys left school to work in the mills, and when they could show the loss of a finger-joint from the machinery they were prized as heroes. The Fourths of July, the Christmases and

Easters and May-Days, which were apparently of greater frequency there and then than they apparently are anywhere now, seemed to alternate with each other through the year, and the Saturdays spread over half the week.

v

The experience of such things was that of the generalized boy, and easy to recall, but the experience of the specialized boy that I was cannot be distinctly recovered and cannot be given in any order of time; the events are like dreams in their achronic simultaneity. I ought to be able to remember when fear first came into my life; but I cannot. I am aware of offering as a belated substitute for far earlier acquaintance with it the awe which I dimly shared with the whole community at a case of hydrophobia occurring there, and which was not lessened by hearing my father tell my mother of the victim's saying: "I have made my peace with God; you may call in the doctors." I doubt if she relished the involuntary satire as he did; his humor, which made life easy for him, could not always have been a comfort to her. Safe in the philosophy of Swedenborg, which taught him that even those who ended in hell chose it their portion because they were happiest in it, he viewed with kindly amusement the religious tumults of the frequent revivals about him. The question of salvation was far below that of the annexation of Texas, or the ensuing war against Mexico, in his regard; but these great events have long ago faded into national history from my contemporary consciousness, while a tragical effect from his playfulness remains vivid in my childish memory. I have already used it in fiction, as my wont has been with so many of my experiences, but I will tell again how my mother and he were walking together in the twilight, with me, a very

22

small boy, following, and my father held out to me behind his back a rose which I understood I was to throw at my mother and startle her.

My aim was unfortunately for me all too sure; the rose struck her head, and when she looked round and saw me offering to run away, she whirled on me and made me suffer for her fright in thinking my flower was a bat, while my father gravely entreated, "Mary, Mary!" She could not forgive me at once, and my heart remained sore, for my love of her was as passionate as the temper I had from her, but while it continued aching after I went to bed, she stole up-stairs to me and consoled me and told me how scared she had been, and hardly knew what she was doing; and all was well again between us.

I wish I could say how dear she was to me and to all her children. My eldest brother and she understood each other best, but each of us lived in the intelligence of her which her love created. She was always working for us, and yet, as I so tardily perceived, living for my father anxiously, fearfully, bravely, with absolute trust in his goodness and righteousness. While she listened to his reading at night, she sewed or knitted for us, or darned or mended the day's ravage in our clothes till, as a great indulgence, we fell asleep on the floor. If it was summer we fell asleep at her knees on the front door-step, where she had sat watching us at our play till we dropped worn out with it; or if it had been a day of wild excess she followed us to our beds early and washed our feet with her dear hands, and soothed them from the bruises of the summer-long shoelessness. She was not only the center of home to me; she was home itself, and in the years before I made a home of my own, absence from her was the homesickness, or the fear of it, which was always haunting me. As for the quick temper (now so slow) I had from her, it showed itself once in a burst of reckless fury which

3   23

had to be signalized in the family rule, so lenient otherwise, by a circumstantial whipping from my father. Another, from her, for going in swimming (as we always said for bathing) when directly forbidden, seems to complete the list of my formal punishments at their hands in a time when fathers and mothers were much more of Solomon's mind in such matters than now.

I never was punished in any sort at school where the frequent scourging of other boys, mostly boys whom I loved for something kind and sweet in them, filled me with anguish; and I have come to believe that a blow struck a child is far wickeder than any wickedness a child can do; that it depraves whoever strikes the blow, mother, or father, or teacher, and that it inexpressibly outrages the young life confided to the love of the race. I know that excuses will be found for it, and that the perpetrator of the outrage will try for consolation in thinking that the child quickly forgets, because its pathetic smiles so soon follow its pathetic tears; but the child does not forget; and no callousing from custom can undo the effect in its soul.

From the stress put upon behaving rather than believing in that home of mine we were made to feel that wicked words were of the quality of wicked deeds, and that when they came out of our mouths they depraved us, unless we took them back. I have not forgotten, with any detail of the time and place, a transgression of this sort which I was made to feel in its full significance. My mother had got supper, and my father was, as he often was, late for it, and while we waited impatiently for him, I came out with the shocking wish that he was dead. My mother instantly called me to account for it, and when my father came she felt bound to tell him what I had said. He could then have done no more than gravely give me the just measure of my offense; and his explanation and forgiveness were the sole event. I did not remain with an exaggerated sense of my sin, though in a child's helplessness I could not urge, if I had imagined urging, that my outburst was merely an aspiration for unbelated suppers, and was of the nature of prayers for rain, which good people cometimes put up regardless of consequences. With his Swedenborgian doctrine of degrees in sin, my father might have thought my wild words prompted by evil spirits, but he would have regarded them as qualitatively rather than quantitatively wicked, and would not have committed the dreadful wrong which elders do a child by giving it a sense of sinning far beyond its worst possible willing. As to conduct his teaching was sometimes of an inherited austerity, but where his own personality prevailed, there was no touch of Puritanism in it.

Our religious instruction at home was not very stated, though it was abundant, and it must have been because we children ourselves felt it unseemly not to go, like other children, to Sunday-school that we were allowed to satisfy our longing for conformity by going for a while to the Sunday-school of the Baptist church, apparently because it was the nearest. We got certain blue tickets and certain red ones for memorizing passages from the New Testament, but I remember much more distinctly the muscular twitching in the close-shaven purplish cheek of the teacher as he nervously listened with set teeth for the children's answers, than anything in our Scripture lessons. I had been received with three or four brothers and sisters into the Swedenborgian communion by a passing New Church minister, but there were no services of our recondite faith in Hamilton, and we shared in no public worship after my mother followed my father from the Methodist society. Out of curiosity and a solemn joy in its ceremonial, I sometimes went to the Catholic church,

where my eyes clung fascinated to the life-large effigy of
Christ bleeding on His cross against the eastern wall; but
I have more present now the sense of walks in the woods
on Sunday, with the whole family, and of the long, sweet
afternoons so spent in them.

If we had no Sabbaths in our house, and not very
recognizable Sundays, we were strictly forbidden to do
anything that would seem to trifle with the scruples of
others. We might not treat serious things unseriously;
we were to swear not at all; and in the matter of bywords
we were allowed very little range, though for the hardness
of our hearts we were suffered to say such things as, "Oh,
hang it!" or even, "Confound it all!" in extreme cases,
such as failing to make the family pony open his mouth
for bridling, or being bitten by the family rabbits, or
butted over by the family goat. In such points of secular
behavior we might be better or worse; but in matters of
religious toleration the rule was inflexible; the faith of
others was sacred, and it was from this early training,
doubtless, that I was able in after life to regard the
occasional bigotry of agnostic friends with toleration.

During the years of my later childhood, a few public
events touched my consciousness. I was much concerned in the fortunes of the Whig party from the candi-
dacy of Henry Clay in 1844 to the fusion of the anti-
slavery Whigs with the Freesoil party after their bolt
of the Taylor nomination in 1848, when I followed my
father as far as a boy of eleven could go. He himself
went so far as to sell his newspaper and take every risk
for the future rather than support a slave-holding candidate who had been chosen for his vote-winning qualities
as a victorious general in the Mexican War. I did not
abhor that aggression so much as my father only because
I could not understand how abhorrent it was; but it
began to be a trouble to me from the first mention of the

YEARS OF MY YOUTH

Annexation of Texas, a sufficiently dismaying mystery, and it afflicted me in early fixing my lot with the righteous minorities which I may have sometimes since been over-proud to be of. Besides such questions of national interest I was aware of other things, such as the French Revolution of 1848; but this must have been wholly through sympathy with my father's satisfaction in the flight of Louis Philippe and the election of the poet Lamartine to be the head of the provisional government. The notion of provisional I relegated to lasting baffle in its more familiar association with the stock of corn-meal and bran in the feed-stores, though I need but have asked in order to be told what it meant. The truth is I was pre-occupied about that time with the affairs of High Olympus, as I imagined them from the mythology which I was reading, and with the politics of Rome and Athens, as I conceived them from the ever-dear histories of Goldsmith. The exploits of the Ingenious Gentleman of La Mancha had much to do in distracting me from the movement of events in Mexico, and at the same time I was enlarging my knowledge of human events through *Gulliver's Travels* and Poe's *Tales of the Grotesque and Arabesque.*

My father had not only explained to me the satire which underlay *Gulliver's Travels;* he told me so much too indignantly of De Foe's appropriation of Selkirk's narrative, that it long kept me from reading *Robinson Crusoe;* but he was, as I have divined more and more, my guide in that early reading which widened with the years, though it kept itself preferably for a long time to history and real narratives. He was of such a liberal mind that he scarcely restricted my own forays in literature, and I think that sometimes he erred on that side; he may have thought no harm could come to me from the literary filth which I sometimes took into my mind, since it was in the nature of sewage to purify itself. He gave

27

me very little direct instruction, and he did not insist
on my going to school when I preferred the printing-
office. All the time, perhaps, I was getting such schooling as came from the love of literature, which was the
daily walk and conversation of our very simple home,
and somehow protected it from the sense of narrow means
and the little hope of larger. My father's income from
his paper was scarcely over a thousand dollars a year,
but this sufficed for his family, then of seven children,
and he was of such a sensitive pride as to money, that
he would hardly ask for debts due him, much less press
for their payment; so that when he parted with his paper
he parted with the hope of much money owing him for
legal and even official advertising and for uncounted delinquent subscriptions. Meanwhile he was earning this
money by the work of his head and hand; and though
I must always love his memory for his proud delicacy,
I cannot forget that this is not a world where people
dun themselves for the debts they owe. What is to be
said of such a man is that his mind is not on the things
that make for prosperity; but if we were in adversity we
never knew it by that name. My mother did the whole
work of her large household, and gave each of us the
same care in health and sickness, in sickness only making
the sufferer feel that he was her favorite; in any other
case she would have felt such a preference wicked. Sometimes she had a hired girl, as people then and there called
the sort of domestic that in New England would have
been called a help. But it must have been very seldom, for two girls alone left record of themselves: a
Dutch girl amusingly memorable with us children because she called her shoes *skoes*, and claimed to have
come to America in a *skip;* and a native girl, who took
charge of us when our mother was on one of her homesick visits Up-the-River, and became lastingly abhorrent
28

for the sort of insipid milk-gravy she made for the beef-steak, and for the nightmare she seemed to have every night, when she filled the house and made our blood run cold with a sort of wild involuntary yodeling.

Apparently my mother's homesickness mounted from time to time in an insupportable crisis; but perhaps she did not go Up-the-River so often as it seemed. She always came back more contented with the home which she herself was for us; once, as my perversely eclectic memory records, it was chiefly because one could burn wood in Hamilton, but had to burn coal at Martin's Ferry, where everything was smutched by it. In my old age, now, I praise Heaven for that home which I could not know apart from her; and I wish I could recall her in the youth which must have been hers when I began to be conscious of her as a personality; I know that she had thick brown Irish hair and blue eyes, and high German cheek-bones, and as a girl she would have had such beauty as often goes with a certain irregularity of feature; but to me before my teens she was, of course, a very mature, if not elderly person, with whom I could not connect any notion of looks except such as shone from her care and love. Though her intellectual and spiritual life was in and from my father, she kept always a certain native quality of speech and a rich sense in words like that which marked her taste in soft stuffs and bright colors. In the hard life of her childhood in the backwoods she was sent to an academy in the nearest town, but in the instant anguish of homesickness she walked ten miles back to the log cabin where at night, as she would tell us, you could hear the wolves howling. She had an innate love of poetry; she could sing some of those songs of Burns and Moore which people sang then. I associate them with her voice in the late summer afternoons; for it was at night that she listened to my father's reading of poetry or fiction. When they were young, before and after their marriage, he kept a book, as people sometimes did in those days, where he wrote in the scrupulous handwriting destined to the deformity of over-use in later years, such poems of Byron or Cowper or Moore or Burns as seemed appropriate to their case, and such other verse as pleased his fancy. It is inscribed (for it still exists) *To Mary,* and with my inner sense I can hear him speaking to her by that sweet name, with the careful English enunciation which separated its syllables into Ma-ry.

VI

My mother was an honored guest on one or other of my uncles' boats whenever she went on her homesick visits Up-the-River, and sometimes we children must have gone with her. Later in my boyhood, when I was nine or ten years old, my father took me to Pittsburg and back, on the boat of the jolliest of those uncles, and it was then that I first fully realized the splendor of the world where their lives were passed. No doubt I have since seen nobler sights than the mile-long rank of the steamboats as they lay at the foot of the landings in the cities at either end of our voyage, but none of these excelling wonders remains like that. All the passenger-boats on the Ohio were then side-wheelers, and their lofty chimneys towering on either side of their pilot-houses were often crenelated at the top, with wire ropes between them supporting the effigies of such Indians as they were named for. From time to time one of the majestic craft pulled from the rank with the clangor of its mighty bell, and the mellow roar of its whistle, and stood out in the yellow stream, or arrived in like state to find a place by the shore. The wide slope of the landing was heaped with the merchandise putting off or taking

on the boats, amidst the wild and whirling curses of the
mates and the insensate rushes of the deck-hands staggering to and fro under their burdens. The swarming
drays came and went with freight, and there were huck-
ster carts of every sort; peddlers, especially of oranges,
escaped with their lives among the hoofs and wheels,
and through the din and turmoil passengers hurried
aboard the boats, to repent at leisure their haste in trust-
ing the advertised hour of departure. It was never
known that any boat left on time, and I doubt if my
uncle's boat, the famous *New England No. 2*, was an
exception to the rule, as my father perfectly understood
while he delayed on the wharf, sampling a book-peddler's
wares, or talking with this bystander or that, while I
waited for him on board in an anguish of fear lest he
should be left behind.

There was a measure of this suffering for me throughout the voyage wherever the boat stopped, for his in-
satiable interest in every aspect of nature and human
nature urged him ashore and kept him there till the last
moment before the gang-plank was drawn in. It was useless for him to argue with me that my uncle would not
allow him to be left, even if he should forget himself so
far as to be in any danger of that. I could not believe
that a disaster so dire should not befall us, and I suffered
a mounting misery till one day it mounted to frenzy. I do
not know whether there were other children on board,
but except for the officers of the boat, I was left mostly
to myself, and I spent my time dreamily watching the
ever-changing shore, so lost in its wild loveliness that
once when I woke from my reverie the boat seemed to
have changed her course, and to be going down-stream
instead of up. It was in this crisis that I saw my father
descending the gang-plank, and while I was urging his
return in mute agony, a boat came up outside of us to
31

wait for her chance of landing. I looked and read on her wheel-house the name *New England*, and then I abandoned hope. By what fell necromancy I had been spirited from my uncle's boat to another I could not guess, but I had no doubt that the thing had happened, and I was flying down from the hurricane roof to leap aboard that boat from the lowermost deck when I met my uncle coming as quietly up the gangway as if nothing had happened. He asked what was the matter, and I gasped out the fact; he did not laugh; he had pity on me and gravely explained, "That boat is the *New England:* this is the *New England No. 2*," and at these words I escaped with what was left of my reason.

I had been the prey of that obsession which every one has experienced when the place where one is disorients itself and west is east and north is south. Sometimes this happens by a sudden trick within the brain, but I lived four years in Columbus and as many in Venice without once being right as to the points of the compass in my nerves, though my wits were perfectly convinced. Once I was months in a place where I suffered from this obsession, when I found myself returning after a journey with the north and south quite where they should be; and, "Now," I exulted, "I will hold them to their duty." I kept my eyes firmly fixed upon the station, as the train approached; then, without my lifting my gaze, the north was back again in the place of the south, and the vain struggle was over. Only the other day I got out of a car going north in Fourth Avenue, and then saw it going on south; and it was only by noting which way the house numbers increased that I could right myself.

I suppose my father promised a reform that should appease my unreason, but whether he could deny himself those chances of general information I am not so sure; we may have both expected too much of each other.

As I was already imaginably interested in things of the mind beyond my years, he often joined me in my perusal of the drifting landscape and made me look at this or that feature of it, but he afterward reported at home that he never could get anything from me but a brief "Yes, indeed," in response. That amused him, yet I do not think I should have disappointed him so much if I could have told him I was losing nothing, but that our point of view was different. The soul of a child is a secret to itself, and in its observance of life there is no foretelling what it shall loose or what it shall hold. I do not believe that anything which was of use to me was lost upon me, but what I chiefly remember now is my pleasure in the log cabins in the woods on the shores, with the blue smoke curling on the morning or the evening air from their chimneys. My heart was taken with a yearning for the wilderness such as the coast-born boy feels for the sea; in the older West the woods called to us with a lure which it would have been rapture to obey; the inappeasable passion for their solitude drove the pioneer into the forest, and it was still in the air we breathed. But my lips were sealed, for the generations cannot utter themselves to each other till the strongest need of utterance is past.

I used to sit a good deal on the hurricane-deck or in the pilot-house, where there was often good talk among the pilots or the boat's officers, and where once I heard with fascination the old Scotch pilot, Tom Lindsay, telling of his own boyhood in the moors, and of the sheep lost in the drifting snows; that also had the charm of the wilderness; but I did not feel the sadness of his saying once, as we drifted past a row of crimson-headed whisky barrels on a wharf-boat, "Many a one of those old Red Eyes I've helped to empty," or imagine the far and deep reach of the words which remained with me. Somewhere in the officers' quarters I found a sea novel, which

I read partly through, but I have not finished *The Cruise
of the Midge*, to this day, though I believe that as sea
novels go it merits reading. When I was not listening to
the talk in the pilot-house, or looking at the hills drifting by, I was watching the white-jacketed black cabin-
boys setting the tables for dinner in the long saloon of
the boat. It was built, after a fashion which still holds
in the Western boats, with a gradual lift of the stem
and stern and a dip midway which somehow enhanced
the charm of the perspective even to the eyes of a hungry
boy. Dinner was at twelve, and the tables began to be
set between ten and eleven, with a rhythmical movement
of the negroes as they added each detail of plates and
cups and knives and glasses, and placed the set dishes
of quivering jelly at discrete intervals under the crystals
of the chandeliers softly tinkling with the pulse of the
engines. At last some more exalted order of waiters
appeared with covered platters and spirit-lamps burning
under them, and set them down before the places of the
captain and his officers. Then the bell was sounded for
the passengers; the waiters leaned forward between these
when they were seated; at a signal from their chief they
lifted the covers of the platters and vanished in a shining procession up the saloon, while each passenger fell
upon the dishes nearest himself.

About the time I had become completely reconciled
to the conditions of the voyage, which the unrivaled
speed of the *New England No. 2* shortened to a three-
days' run up the river, I woke one morning to find her
lying at the Pittsburg landing, and when I had called my
father to come and share my wonder at a stretch of boats
as long as that at Cincinnati, and been mimicked by a
cabin-boy for my unsophisticated amazement, nothing
remained for me but to visit the houses of the aunts
and uncles abounding in cousins. Of the homeward voy-

age nothing whatever is left in my memory; but I know we came back on the *New England No. 2*, though we must have left the boat and taken it again on a second trip at Wheeling, after a week spent with my mother's people at Martin's Ferry. My father wished me to see the glass-foundries and rolling-mills which interested him so much more than me; he could not get enough of those lurid industries which I was chiefly concerned in saving myself from. I feigned an interest in the processes out of regard for him, but Heaven knows I cared nothing for the drawing of wire or the making of nails, and only a very little for the blowing of the red, vitreous bubbles from the mouths of long steel pipes. With weariness I escaped from these wonders, but with no such misery as I eluded the affection of the poor misshapen, half-witted boy who took a fancy to me at the house of some old friends of my father where we had supper after the long day. With uncouth noises of welcome, and with arms and legs flying controllessly about, he followed me through a day that seemed endless. His family of kindly English folk, from the life-long habit of him, seemed unaware of anything strange, and I could not for shame and for fear of my father's reproach betray my suffering. The evening began unduly to fall, thick with the blackness of the coal smoke poured from the chimneys of those abhorred foundries, and there was a fatal moment when my father's friends urged him to stay the night and I thought he would consent. The dreams of childhood are oftenest evil, but mine holds record of few such nightmares as this.

VII

After my father sold his paper and was casting about for some other means of livelihood, there were occasional shadows cast by his anxieties in the bright air of my childhood. Again I doubt if any boy ever lived a gladder time than I lived in Hamilton, Butler County, Ohio: words that I write still when I try a new pen, because I learned to write them first, and love them yet. When we went to live in Dayton, where my father managed to make a sort of progressive purchase of a newspaper which he never quite paid for, our skies changed. It was after an interval of experiment in one sort and another, which amused his hopeful ingenuity, but ended in nothing, that he entered upon this long failure. The Dayton *Transcript* when he began with it was a tri-weekly, but he made it a daily, and this mistake infected the whole enterprise. It made harder work for us all than we had known before; and the printing-office, which had been my delight, became my oppression after the brief moment of public schooling which I somehow knew. But before the change from tri-weekly to daily in our paper, I had the unstinted advantage of a school of morals as it then appeared among us.

The self-sacrificing company of players who suffered for the drama through this first summer of our life in Dayton paid my father for their printing in promises which he willingly took at their face value, and in tickets which were promptly honored at the door. As nearly as I can make out, I was thus enabled to go every night to the theater, in a passion for it which remains with me ardent still. I saw such plays of Shakespeare as "Macbeth" and "Othello," then the stage favorites, and "Richard III." and evermore "Richard III." I saw such other now quite forgotten favorites as Kotzebue's "Stranger" and Sheridan Knowles's "Wife," and such moving actions of unknown origin as "Barbarossa" and "The Miser of Marseilles," with many screaming farces such as helped fill every evening full with at least three

36

plays. There was also at that time a native drama almost as acceptable to our public everywhere as "Uncle Tom's Cabin" afterward became. It seemed as if our public would never tire of "A Glance at New York," with its horribly vulgar stage conceptions of local character, Mose the fireman and Lize his girl, and Sikesy and their other companions, which drift up before me now like wraiths from the Pit, and its events of street-fighting and I dare say heroic rescues from burning buildings by the volunteer fire companies of the day. When it appeared that the public might tire of the play, the lively fancy of the theater supplied a fresh attraction in it, and the character of Little Mose was added. How this must have been played by what awful young women eager to shine at any cost in their art, I shudder to think, and it is with "sick and scornful looks averse" that I turn from the remembrance of my own ambition to shine in that drama. My father instantly quenched the histrionic spark in me with loathing; but I cannot say whether this was before or after the failure of a dramatic attempt of his own which I witnessed, much mystified by the sense of some occult relation to it. Certainly I did not know that the melodrama which sacrificed his native to his adoptive patriotism in the action, and brought off the Americans victors over the British in a sea-fight, was his work; and probably it was the adaptation of some tale then much read. Very likely he trusted, in writing it, to the chance which he always expected to favor the amateur in taking up a musical instrument strange to him. He may even have dreamed of fortune from it; but after one performance of it the management seems to have gone back to such old public favorites as Shakespeare and Sheridan Knowles. Nothing was said of it in the family; I think some of the newspapers were not so silent; but I am not sure of this.

My father could, of course, be wiser for others than for himself; the public saved him from becoming a dramatist, but it was he who saved me from any remotest chance of becoming an actor, and later from acquiring the art of the prestidigitator. The only book which I can be sure of his taking from me was a manual professing to teach this art, which I had fallen in with. The days of those years in Dayton were in fact very different from the days in Hamilton when I was reaching out near and far to feed my fancy for fable and my famine for fact. I read no new books which now occur to me by name, though I still kept my interest in Greek mythology and gave something of my scanty leisure to a long poem in the quatrains of Gray's Elegy based upon some divine event of it. The course of the poem was lastingly arrested by a slight attack of the cholera which was then raging in the town and filling my soul with gloom. My dear mother thought it timely to speak with me of the other world; but so far from reconciling me to the thought of it, I suppose she could not have found a boy in all Dayton more unwilling to go to heaven. She was forced to drop her religious consolations and to assure me that she had not the least fear of my dying.

It was certainly not the fault of the place that we were, first and last, rather unhappy there. For one thing, we were used to the greater ease and simplicity of a small town like Hamilton, and Dayton was a small city with the manners and customs of cities in those days: that is, there was more society and less neighborhood, and neither my father nor my mother could have cared for society. They missed the wont of old friends; there were no such teas as she used to give her neighbors, with a quilting, still dimly visioned, at the vanishing-point of the perspective; our social life was almost wholly in our Sunday-evening visits to the house of my young aunt whose husband was my father's youngest brother. The pair were already in the shadow of their early death, and in the sorrow of losing their children one after another till one little cousin alone remained. I had not yet begun to make up romances about people in my mind, but this uncle and aunt were my types of worldly splendor in the setting of the lace curtains and hair-cloth chairs of their parlor, with her piano and his flute for other æsthetic grace. He was so much younger that he had a sort of filial relation to my father, and they were both very sweet to my mother, always lonely outside of her large family.

As usual, we lived in more than one house, but the first was very acceptable because of its nearness to the canal; the yard stretched behind it quite to the tow-path, with an unused stable between, which served us boys for circus-rehearsals, and for dressing after a plunge. As in a dream, I can still see my youngest brother rushing through this stable one day and calling out that he was going to jump into the canal, with me running after him and then dimly seeing him as he groped along the bottom, with me diving and saving him from drowning. Already, with the Hamilton facilities, I could hardly help being a good swimmer, and at Dayton I spent much of my leisure in the canal. Within the city limits we had to wear some sort of bathing-dress, and we preferred going with a crowd of other boys beyond the line where no such formality was expected of us. On the way to and fro we had to pass a soap-factory, where the boys employed in it swarmed out at sight of us stealing along under the canal bank, and in the strange outlawry of boyhood murderously stoned us, but somehow did not kill us. I do not know what boys we played with, but after we had paid the immemorial penalty of the stranger, and fought for our standing among them, the boys of our neighborhood were kind enough. One, whose father was a tobacconist,

4

39

abetted our efforts to learn smoking by making cigars flavored with cinnamon-drops; I suppose these would have been of more actual advantage to me if I had learned to like smoking. When we went from his house to another, in what may have been a better quarter, we made no friends that I can remember, and we were never so gay. In fact, a sense of my father's adversity now began to penetrate to his older children, with the knowledge of our mother's unhappiness from it.

I am not following any chronological order here, and I should not be able to date my æsthetic devotion to a certain gas-burner in the window of a store under the printing-office. It was in the form of a calla-lily, with the flame forking from the tongue in its white cup; and I could never pass it, by day or night, without stopping to adore it. If I could be perfectly candid, I should still own my preference of it to the great painting of Adam and Eve by Dubuffe, then shown throughout our simple-hearted commonwealth. This had the double attraction of a religious interest and the awful novelty of the nude, for the first time seen by untraveled American eyes; the large canvas was lighted up so as to throw the life-size figures into strong relief, and the spectator strickenly studied them through a sort of pasteboard binocle supplied for the purpose. If that was the way our first parents looked before the Fall, and the Bible said it was, there was nothing to be urged against it; but many kind people must have suffered secret misgivings at a sight from which a boy might well shrink ashamed, with a feeling that the taste of Eden was improved by the Fall. I had no such joy in it as in the dramas which I witnessed in the same hall; as yet there was nothing in Dayton openly declared a theater.

The town had many airs of a city, and there were even some policemen who wore a silver-plated star inside their coats for proof of their profession. There were water-works, and there was gas everywhere for such as would pay the charge for it. My father found the expense of piping the printing-office too great for his means, or else he preferred falling back upon his invention, and instead of the usual iron tubes he had the place fitted with tin tubes, at much less cost. Perhaps the cost was equalized in the end by the leaking of these tubes, which was so constant that we breathed gas by day as well as burned it by night. We burned it a good deal, for our tri-weekly was now changed to a daily, and a morning paper at that. Until eleven o'clock I helped put the telegraphic de-spatches (then a new and proud thing with us) into type, and between four and five o'clock in the morning I was up and carrying papers to our subscribers. The stress of my father's affairs must have been very sore for him to allow this, and I dare say it did not last long, but while it lasted it was suffering which must make me forever ten-der of those who overwork, especially the children who overwork. The suffering was such that when my brother, who had not gone to bed till much later, woke me after my five or six hours' sleep, I do not now know how I got myself together for going to the printing-office for the papers and making my rounds in the keen morning air. When Sunday came, and I could sleep as late as I liked, it was bliss such as I cannot tell to lie and rest, and rest, and rest! We were duteous children and willing; my brother knew of the heavy trouble hanging over us and I was aware of the hopeless burden of debt which our father was staggering under and my mother was carry-ing on her heart; and when I think of it, and of the wide-spread, never-ending struggle for life which it was and is the type of, I cannot but abhor the economic condi-tions which we still suppose an essential of civilization.

Lest these facts should make too vivid a call upon the

reader's compassion, I find it advisable to remember here
an instance of hard-heartedness in me which was worthier
the adamantine conscience of some full-grown moralist
than a boy of my age. There was a poor girl, whose
misfortune was known to a number of families where she
was employed as a seamstress, and the more carefully
treated because of her misfortune. Among others my
mother was glad to give her work; and she lived with
us like one of ourselves, of course sitting at table with
us and sharing in such family pleasures as we knew. She
was the more to be pitied because her betrayer was a
prominent man who bore none of the blame for their
sin; but when her shame became known to me I began
a persecution of the poor creature in the cause of social
purity. I would not take a dish from her at table, or hand
her one; I would not speak to her, if I could help it, or
look at her; I left the room when she came into it; and
I expressed by every cruelty short of words my righteous condemnation. I was, in fact, society incarnate in
the attitude society takes toward such as she. Heaven
knows how I came by such a devilish ideal of propriety,
and I cannot remember how the matter quite ended, but
I seem to remember a crisis, in which she begged my
mother with tears to tell her why I treated her so; and
I was put to bitter shame for it. It could not be explained to me how tragical her case was; I must have
been thought too young for the explanation; but I doubt
if any boy of twelve is too young for the right knowledge of such things; he already has the wrong.

My wish at times to learn some other business was
indulged by a family council, and my uncle made a
place for me in his drug-store, where, as long as the novelty
lasted, I was happy in the experiments with chemicals
permitted to me and a fellow-apprentice. Mainly we
were busied in putting up essence of peppermint and pare-

goric and certain favorite medicinal herbs; and when the first Saturday evening came, my companion received his weekly wage over the counter, and I expected mine, but the bookkeeper smiled and said he would have to see my uncle about that; in the end, it appeared that by the convention with my father I was somehow not to draw any salary. Both my uncle and he treated the matter with something of the bookkeeper's smiling slight, and after an interval, now no longer appreciable, I found myself in the printing-office again. I was not sorry, and yet I had liked the drug business so far as I had gone in it, and I liked that old bookkeeper, though he paid me no money. How, after a life of varied experiences, he had lodged at last in the comfortable place he held I no longer know, if I ever knew. He had been at one time what would once have been called a merchant adventurer in various seas; and he had been wrecked on the Galapagos Islands, where he had feasted on the famous native turtle, now extinct, with a relish which he still smacked his lips in remembering.

This episode, which I cannot date, much antedated the period of my father's business failure, though his struggles against it must have already begun; they began, in fact, from the moment of his arrival in Dayton, and the freest and happiest hours we knew there were when the long strain ended in the inevitable break. Then there was an interval, I do not know how great, but perhaps of months, when there was a casting about for some means of living, and to this interval belongs somehow the employment of my brother and myself in a German printing-office, such as used to be found in every considerable Ohio town. I do not know what we did there, but I remember the kindly German printer-folk, and the merry times we had with them, in the smoke of their pipes and the warmth of their stove heated red against the autumnal cold. I explore my memory in vain for proof that my father had some job-printing interest in this German office, but I remember my interest in the German type and its difference from the English. I was yet far from any interest in the German poetry which afterward became one of my passions, and there is no one now left alive whom I can ask whether the whole incident was fact, or not, rather, the sort of dream which all the past becomes when we try to question it.

What I am distinctly aware of, through a sense of rather sullen autumnal weather, is that a plan for our going into the country evolved itself in full detail between my father and uncle. My uncle was to supply the capital for the venture, and was finally, with two other uncles, to join my father on a milling privilege which they had bought at a point on the Little Miami River, where all the families were to be settled. In the mean time my father was to have charge of a grist-mill and sawmill on the property till they could be turned into a paper-mill and a sort of communal settlement of suitable people could be gathered. He had never run a sawmill or a grist-mill, much less evoked a paper-mill from them; but neither had he ever gathered a community of choice spirits for the enjoyment of a social form which enthusiasts like Robert Owen had dreamed into being, and then non-being, in the Middle West in those or somewhat earlier days. What was definite and palpable in the matter was that he must do something, and that he had the heart and hope for the experiment.

VIII

I have told the story of this venture in a little book called *My Year in a Log Cabin*, printed twenty-odd years ago, and I cannot do better now than let it rehearse itself here from those pages, with such slight change or none as insists. For my father, whose boyhood had been passed in the new country, where pioneer customs and traditions were still rife, it was like renewing the wild romance of those days to take up once more the life in a log cabin interrupted by many years' sojourn in matter-of-fact dwellings of frame and brick. It was the fond dream of his boys to realize the trials and privations which he had painted for them in rosy hues, and even if the only clapboarded dwelling at the mills had not been occupied by the miller, we should have disdained it for the log cabin which we made our home till we could build a new house.

Our cabin stood close upon the road, but behind it broadened a corn-field of eighty acres. They still built log cabins for dwellings in that region at the time, but ours must have been nearly half a century old when we went into it. It had been recently vacated by an old poor-white Virginian couple, who had long occupied it, and we decided that it needed some repairs to make it habitable even for a family inured to hardship by dauntless imaginations, and accustomed to retrospective discomforts of every kind.

So before the family all came out to it a deputation of adventurers put it in what rude order they could. They glazed the narrow windows, they relaid the rotten floor, they touched (too sketchily, as it afterward appeared) the broken roof, and they papered the walls of the ground-floor rooms. Perhaps it was my father's love of literature which inspired him to choose newspapers for this purpose; at any rate, he did so, and the effect, as I remember, had its decorative qualities. He had used a barrel of papers from the nearest post-office, where they had been refused by people to whom they had been experimentally sent by the publishers, and the whole first page was taken up by a story, which broke off in the middle of a sentence at the foot of the last column, and tantalized us forever with fruitless conjecture as to the fate of the hero and heroine.

The cabin, rude as it was, was not without its sophistications, its concessions to the spirit of modern luxury. The logs it was built of had not been left rounded, as they grew, but had been squared in a sawmill, and the crevices between them had not been chinked with moss and daubed with clay in true backwoods fashion, but plastered with mortar, and the chimney, instead of being a structure of clay-covered sticks, was laid in courses of stone. Within, however, it was all that could be desired by the most romantic of pioneer families. It was six feet wide and a yard deep, its cavernous maw would easily swallow a back-log eighteen inches through, and we piled in front the sticks of hickory cord-wood as high as we liked. We made a perfect trial of it when we came out to put the cabin in readiness for the family, and when the hickory had dropped into a mass of tinkling, snapping, bristling embers we laid our rashers of bacon and our slices of steak upon them, and tasted the flavors of the wildwood in the captured juices. At night we laid our mattresses on the sweet new oak plank of the floor, and slept hard—in every sense.

In due time the whole family took up its abode in the cabin. The household furniture had been brought out and bestowed in its scanty space, the bookcase had been set up, and the unbound books left easily accessible in barrels. There remained some of our possessions to follow, chief of which was the cow; for in those simple days people kept cows in town, and it fell to me to help my father drive ours out to her future home. We got on famously, talking of the wayside things so beautiful in the autumnal day, panoplied in the savage splendor of its painted leaves, and of the books and authors so dear to the boy who limped barefooted by his father's side, with

46

his eye on the cow and his mind on Cervantes and Shake-speare. But the cow was very slow—far slower than the boy's thoughts—and it had fallen night and was already thick dark when we had made the twelve miles and stood under the white-limbed phantasmal sycamores beside the tail-race of the grist-mill, and questioned how we should get across with our charge. We did not know how deep the water was, but we knew it was very cold, and we would rather not wade it. The only thing to do seemed to be for one of us to run up to the sawmill, cross the head-race there, and come back to receive the cow on the other side of the tail-race. But the boy could not bring himself either to go or to stay.

The kind-hearted father urged, but he would not com-pel; you cannot well use force with a boy when you have been talking literature and philosophy for half a day with him. We could see the lights in the cabin cheer-fully twinkling, and we shouted to those within, but no one heard us. We called and called in vain. Nothing but the cold rush of the tail-race, the dry rustle of the syca-more-leaves, and the homesick lowing of the cow replied. We determined to drive her across, and pursue her with sticks and stones through the darkness beyond, and then run at the top of our speed to the sawmill, and get back to take her in custody again. We carried out our part of the plan perfectly, but the cow had not entered into it with intelligence or sympathy. When we reached the other side of the tail-race again she was nowhere to be found, and no appeals of "Boss" or "Suky" or "Suboss" availed. She must have instantly turned, and retraced, in the darkness which seemed to have swallowed her up, the weary steps of the day, for she was found in her old home in town the next morning. At any rate, she had abandoned the father to the conversation of his son, for the time being, and the son had nothing to say.

I do not remember now just how it was that we came by the different "animals of the horse kind," as my father called them, which we housed in an old log stable not far from our cabin. They must have been a temporary supply until a team worthy our new sky-blue wagon could be found. One of them was a colossal sorrel, inexorably hide-bound, whose barrel, as horsemen call the body, showed every hoop upon it. He had a feeble, foolish whimper of a voice, and we nicknamed him "Baby." His companion was a dun mare, who had what my father at once called an italic foot, in recognition of the emphatic slant at which she carried it when upon her unwilling travels. Then there was a small, self-opinionated gray pony, which was of no service conjecturable after this lapse of time. We boys rode him barebacked, and he used to draw a buggy, which he finally ran away with. I suppose we found him useful in the representation of some of the Indian fights which we were always dramatizing, and I dare say he may have served our turn as an Arab charger, when the Moors of Granada made one of their sallies upon the camp of the Spaniards, and discharged their javelins into it; their javelins were the long, admirably straight and slender ironweeds that grew by the river. This menagerie was constantly breaking bounds and wandering off; and was chiefly employed in hunting itself up, its different members taking turns in remaining in the pasture or stable, to be ridden after those that had strayed into the woods.

The origin of a large and eloquent flock of geese is lost in an equal obscurity. I recall their possession simply as an accomplished fact, and I associate their desolate cries with the windy dark of rainy November nights, so that they must at least have come into our hands after the horses. They were fenced into a clayey area next the cabin for safe-keeping, where, perpetually waddling about in a majestic disoccupation, they patted the damp ground down to the hardness and smoothness of a brick-yard. Throughout the day they conversed tranquilly together, but by night they woke, goose after goose, to send forth a long clarion alarum, blending in a general concert at last, to assure one another of their safety. We must have intended to pluck them in the spring, but they stole their nests early in March, and entered upon the nurture of their young before we could prevent it; and it would then have been barbarous to pluck these mothers of families.

We had got some pigs from our old Virginian predecessors, and these kept, as far as they could, the domestic habits in which that affectionate couple had indulged them. They would willingly have shared our fireside with us, humble as it was, but, being repelled, they took up their quarters on cold nights at the warm base of the chimney without, where we could hear them, as long as we kept awake, disputing the places next to the stones. All this was horrible to my mother, whose housewifely instincts were perpetually offended by the rude conditions of our life, and who justly regarded it as a return to a state which, if poetic, was also not far from barbaric. But boys take every natural thing as naturally as savages, and we never thought our pigs were other than amusing. In that country pigs were called to their feed with long cries of "Pig, pig, pooee, poe-e-e!" but ours were taught to come at a whistle, and, on hearing it, would single themselves out from the neighbors' pigs, and come rushing from all quarters to the scattered corn with an intelligence we were proud of.

IX

As long as the fall weather lasted, and well through the mild winter of that latitude, our chief recreation, where all our novel duties were delightful, was hunting with the long, smooth-bore shot-gun which had descended laterally from one of our uncles, and supplied the needs of the whole family of boys in the chase. Never less than two of us went out with it at once, and generally there were three. This enabled us to beat up the game over a wide extent of country, and while the eldest did the shooting, left the others to rush upon him as soon as he fired, with tumultuous cries of, "Did you hit it? Did you hit it?" We fell upon the wounded squirrels which we brought down on rare occasions, and put them to death with what I must now call a sickening ferocity. If sometimes the fool dog, the weak-minded Newfoundland pup we were rearing, rushed upon the game first, and the squirrel avenged his death upon the dog's nose, that was pure gain, and the squirrel had the applause of his other enemies. Yet we were none of us cruel; we never wantonly killed things that could not be eaten; we should have thought it sacrilege to shoot a robin or a turtle-dove, but we were willing to be amused, and these were the chances of war.

The woods were full of squirrels, which especially abounded in the woods-pastures, as we called the lovely dells where the greater part of the timber was thinned out to let the cattle range and graze. They were of all sorts—gray, and black, and even big red fox-squirrels, a variety I now suppose extinct. When the spring opened we hunted them in the poplar woods, whither they resorted in countless numbers for the sweetness in the cups of the tulip-tree blossoms. I recall with a thrill one memorable morning in such woods—early, after an overnight rain, when the vistas hung full of a delicate mist that the sun pierced to kindle a million fires in the drops still pendulous from leaf and twig. I can smell the tulip-blossoms and the odor of the tree-bark yet, and the fresh, strong fragrance of the leafy mold under my bare feet; and I can hear the rush of the squirrels on the bark of the trunks, or the swish of their long, plunging leaps from bough to bough in the air-tops.

In a region where the corn-fields and wheat-fields were often fifty and sixty acres in extent there was a plenty of quail, but I remember only one victim to my gun. We set figure-four traps to catch them; but they were shrewder arithmeticians than we, and solved these problems without harm to themselves. When they began to mate, and the air was full of their soft, amorous whistling, we searched for their nests, and had better luck, though we were forbidden to rob the nests when we found them; and in June, when a pretty little mother strutted across the lanes at the head of her tiny brood, we had to content ourselves with the near spectacle of her cunning counterfeit of disability at sight of us, fluttering and tumbling in the dust till her chicks could hide themselves. We had read of that trick, and were not deceived; but we were charmed the same.

It is a trick that all birds know, and I had it played upon me by the mother snipe and mother wild duck that haunted our dam, as well as by the quail. With the snipe, once, I had a fancy to see how far the mother would carry the ruse, and so ran after her; but in doing this I trod on one of her young—a soft, gray mite, not distinguishable from the gray pebbles where it ran. I took it tenderly up in my hand, and it is a pang to me yet to think how it gasped once and died. A boy is a strange mixture—as the man who comes after him is. I should not have minded knocking over that whole brood of snipes with my gun, if I could; but this poor little death was somehow very personal in its appeal.

I had no such regrets concerning the young wild ducks, which, indeed, I had no such grievous accident with.

51

I left their mother to flounder and flutter away as she would, and took to the swamp where her young sought refuge from me. There I spent half a day wading about in waters that were often up to my waist and full of ugly possibilities of mud-turtles and water-snakes, trying to put my hand on one of the ducklings. They rose everywhere else, and dived again after a breath of air; but at last one of them came up in my very grasp. It did not struggle, but how its wild heart bounded against my hand! I carried it home to show it and boast of my capture, and then I took it back to its native swamp. It dived instantly, and I hope it found its bereaved family somewhere under the water.

The center of our life in the cabin was, of course, the fireplace, whose hugeness and whose mighty fires remained a wonder with us. There was a crane in the chimney and dangling pot-hooks, and until the cooking-stove could be set up in an adjoining shed the cooking had to be done on the hearth, and the bread baked in a Dutch oven in the hot ashes. We had always heard of this operation, which was a necessity of early days; and nothing else, perhaps, realized them so vividly for us as the loaf laid in the iron-lidded skillet, which was then covered with ashes and heaped with coals.

I am not certain that the bread tasted any better for the historical romance of its experience, or that the corn-meal, mixed warm from the mill and baked on an oak plank set up before the fire, had merits beyond the hoe-cake of art; but I think there can be no doubt that new corn grated from the cob while still in the milk, and then molded and put in like manner to brown in the glow of such embers, would still have the sweetness that was incomparable then. When the maple sap started in February, we tried the scheme we had cherished all winter of making with it tea which should be in a manner self-sugared. But the scheme was a failure—we spoiled the sap without sweetening the tea.

We sat up late before the big fire at night, our faces burning in the glow, and our backs and feet freezing in the draught that swept in from the imperfectly closing door, and then we boys climbed to our bed in the loft. We reached it by a ladder, which we should have been glad to pull up after us as a protection against Indians in the pioneer fashion; but, with the advancement of modern luxury, the ladder had been nailed to the floor. When we were once aloft, however, we were in a domain sacred to the past. The rude floor rattled and wavered loosely under our tread, and the window in the gable stood open or shut at its own will. There were cracks in the shingles, through which we could see the stars, when there were stars, and which, when the first snow came, let the flakes sift in upon the floor.

Our barrels of paper-covered books were stowed away in that loft, and, overhauling them one day, I found a paper copy of the poems of a certain Henry W. Longfellow, then wholly unknown to me; and while the old grist-mill, whistling and wheezing to itself, made a vague music in my ears, my soul was filled with this new, strange sweetness. I read the "Spanish Student" there, and the "Coplas de Manrique," and the solemn and ever-beautiful "Voices of the Night." There were other books in those barrels, but these spirited me again to Spain, where I had already been with Irving, and led me to attack fitfully the old Spanish grammar which had been knocking about our house ever since my father bought it from a soldier of the Mexican War.

But neither these nor any other books made me discontented with the boy's world about me. They made it a little more populous with visionary shapes, but that was well, and there was room for them all. It was not

53

darkened with cares, and the duties of it were not many. By this time we older boys had our axes, and believed ourselves to be clearing a piece of woods which covered a hill belonging to the milling property. The timber was black-walnut and oak and hickory, and I cannot think we made much inroad in it; but we must have felled some of the trees, for I remember helping to cut them into saw-logs with the cross-cut saw, and the rapture we had in starting our logs from the brow of the hill and watching their whirling rush to the bottom. We experimented, as boys will, and we felled one large hickory with the saw instead of the axe, and scarcely escaped with our lives when it suddenly split near the bark, and the butt shot out between us. I preferred buckeye and sycamore trees for my own axe; they were of no use when felled, but they chopped so easily.

They grew abundantly on the island which formed another feature of our oddly distributed property. This island was by far its most fascinating feature, and for us boys it had the charm and mystery which have in every land and age endeared islands to the heart of man. It was not naturally an island, but had been made so by the mill-races bringing the water from the dam, and emptying into the river again below the mills. It was flat, and half under water in every spring freshet, but it had precious areas grown up to tall ironweeds, which, withering and hardening in the frost, supplied us with the darts for our Indian fights. The island was always our battle-ground, and it resounded in the long afternoons with the war-cries of the encountering tribes. We had a book in those days called *Western Adventure*, which was made up of tales of pioneer and frontier life, and we were constantly reading ourselves back into that life. This book, and Howe's *Collections for the History of Ohio*, were full of stories of the backwoodsmen and warriors who had made our state a battle-ground for nearly fifty years, and our life in the log cabin gave new zest to the tales of "Simon Kenton, the Pioneer," and "Simon Girty, the Renegade"; of the captivity of Crawford, and his death at the stake; of the massacre of the Moravian Indians at Gnadenhütten; of the defeat of St. Clair and the victory of Wayne; of a hundred other wild and bloody incidents of our annals. We read of them at night till we were afraid to go up the ladder to the ambuscade of savages in our loft, but we fought them over by day with undaunted spirit. With our native romance I sometimes mingled from my own reading a strain of Old World poetry, and "Hamet el Zegri" and the "Unknown Spanish Knight," encountered in the Vega before Granada on our island, while Adam Poe and the Indian chief Bigfoot were taking breath from their deadly struggle in the waters of the Ohio.

X

When the spring opened we broke up the sod on a more fertile part of the island, and planted a garden there beside our field of corn. We planted long rows of sweet-potatoes, and a splendid profusion of melons, which duly came up with their empty seed-shells fitted like helmets over their heads, and were mostly laid low the next day by the cutworms wh ch swarmed in the upturned sod. But the sweet-potatoes had better luck. Better luck I did not think it then; their rows seemed interminable to a boy set to clear them of purslane with his hoe; though I do not now imagine they were necessarily a day's journey in length. Neither could the corn-field beside them have been very vast; but again reluctant boyhood has a different scale for the measurement of such things, and perhaps if I were now set to hill it up I might think differently about its size.

5   55

I dare say it was not well cared for, but an inexhaustible wealth of ears came into the milk just at the right moment for our enjoyment. We had then begun to build our new house, and for this we were now kiln-drying the green oak flooring-boards. We had built a long skeleton hut, and had set the boards upright all around it and roofed it with them, and in the middle of it we had set a huge old cast-iron stove, in which we kept a roaring fire. The fire had to be watched night and day, and it often took all the boys of the neighborhood to watch it, and to turn the boards. It must have been cruelly hot in that kiln; but I remember nothing of that; I remember only the luxury of the green corn, spitted on the points of long sticks and roasted in the red-hot stove; we must almost have roasted our own heads at the same time. But I suppose that if the heat within the kiln or without ever became intolerable, we escaped from it and from our light summer clothing, reduced to a Greek simplicity, in a delicious plunge in the river. We had our choice of the shallows, where the long ripple was warmed through and through by the sun in which it sparkled, or the swimming-hole, whose depths were almost as tepid, but were here and there interwoven with mysterious cool under-currents.

We believed that there were snapping-turtles and water-snakes in our swimming-holes, though we never saw any. There were some fish in the river, chiefly suckers and catfish in the spring, when the water was high and turbid, and in summer the bream that we call sunfish in the West, and there was a superstition, never verified by us, of bass. We did not care much for fishing, though of course that had its turn in the pleasures of our rolling year. There were crawfish, both hard-shell and soft, to be had at small risk, and mussels in plenty. Their shells furnished us the material for many rings zealously begun and never finished; we did not see why they did not pro-

duce pearls; but perhaps they were all eaten up, before
the pearl disease could attack them, by the muskrats,
before whose holes their shells were heaped.

Of skating on the river I think we had none. The
winter often passed in our latitude without making ice
enough for that sport, and there could not have been
much sledding, either. We read, enviously enough, in
Peter Parley's *First Book of History*, of the coasting on
Boston Common, and we made some weak-kneed sleds
(whose imbecile runners flattened helplessly under them)
when the light snows began to come; but we never had
any real coasting, as our elders never had any real sleighing in the jumpers they made by splitting a hickory sap-
ling for runners, and mounting any sort of rude box upon
them. They might have used sleighs in the mud, however; that was a foot deep on most of the roads, and
lasted all winter. For a little while some of us went
two miles away through the woods to school; but there
was not much to be taught a reading family like ours in
that log hut, and I suppose it was not thought worth
while to keep us at it. No impression of it remains to
me, except the wild, lonesome cooing of the turtle-doves
when they began to nest in the neighboring oaks.

Our new house got on slowly. The log cabin had not
become pleasanter with the advance of the summer, and
we looked forward to our occupation of the new house
with an eagerness which even in us boys must have had
some sense of present discomfort at the bottom of it.
The frame was of oak, and my father decided to have the
house weather-boarded and shingled with black-walnut,
which was so much cheaper than pine, and which, left
in its natural state, he thought would be agreeable in color.
It appeared to me a palace. I spent all the leisure I
had from swimming and Indian-fighting and reading in
watching the carpenter work, and hearing him talk; his

talk was not the wisest, but he thought very well of it himself, and I had so far lapsed from civilization that I stood in secret awe of him, because he came from town—from the little village, namely, two miles away.

I try to give merely a child's memories of our life, which were nearly all delightful; but it must have been hard for my elders, and for my mother especially, who could get no help, or only briefly and fitfully, in the work that fell to her. Now and then a New Church minister, of those who used to visit us in town, passed a Sunday with us in the cabin, and that was a rare time of mental and spiritual refreshment for her. Otherwise, my father read us a service out of the *Book of Worship*, or a chapter from the *Heavenly Arcana;* and week-day nights, while the long evenings lasted, he read poetry to us—Scott, or Moore, or Thomson, or some of the more didactic poets.

In the summer evenings, after her long hard day's work was done, my mother sometimes strolled out upon the island with my father, and loitered on the bank to look at her boys in the river; one such evening I recall, and how sad our gay voices were in the dim, dewy air. My father had built a flatboat, which we kept on the smooth waters of our dam, and on Sunday afternoons the whole family went out in it. We rowed far up, till we struck a current from the mill above us, and then let the boat drift slowly down again. It does not now seem very exciting, but then to a boy whose sense was open to every intimation of beauty, the silence that sang in our ears, the stillness of the dam where the low uplands and the fringing sycamores and every rush and grass-blade by the brink perfectly glassed themselves with the vast blue sky overhead, were full of mystery, of divine promise, and holy awe.

I recollect the complex effort of these Sunday afternoons as if they were all one sharp event; I recall in like manner the starry summer nights, and there is one of these nights that remains single and peerless in my memory. My brother and I had been sent on an errand to some neighbor's—for a bag of potatoes or a joint of meat; it does not matter—and we had been somehow belated, so that it was well after twilight when we started home, and the round moon was high when we stopped to rest in a piece of the lovely open woodland of that region, where the trees stood in a parklike freedom from underbrush, and the grass grew dense and rich among them. We took the pole, on which we had slung the bag, from our shoulders, and sat down on an old long-fallen log, and listened to the densely interwoven monotonies of the innumerable katydids, in which the air seemed clothed as with a mesh of sound. The shadows fell black from the trees upon the smooth sward, but every other place was full of the tender light in which all forms were rounded and softened; the moon hung tranced in the sky. We scarcely spoke in the shining solitude, the solitude which for once had no terrors for the childish fancy, but was only beautiful. This perfect beauty seemed not only to liberate me from the fear which is the prevailing mood of childhood, but to lift my soul nearer and nearer to the soul of all things in an exquisite sympathy. Such moments never pass; they are ineffaceable; their rapture immortalizes; from them we know that, whatever perishes, there is something in us that cannot die, that divinely regrets, divinely hopes.

XI

Our log cabin stood only a stone's-cast from the gray old weather-tinted grist-mill, whose voice was music for us by night and by day, so that on Sundays, when the water was shut off from the great tub-wheels in its basement, it was as if the world had gone deaf and dumb. A soft sibilance prevailed by day over the dull, hoarse murmur of the machinery; but late at night, when the water gathered that mysterious force which the darkness gives it, the voice of the mill had something weird in it like a human moan.

It was in all ways a place which I did not care to explore alone. It was very well, with a company of boys, to tumble and wrestle in the vast bins full of tawny wheat, or to climb the slippery stairs to the cooling-floor in the loft, whither the little pockets of the elevators carried the meal warm from the burrs, and the blades of the wheel up there, worn smooth by years of use, spread it out in an ever-widening circle, and caressed it with a thousand repetitions of their revolution. But the heavy rush of the water upon the wheels in the dim, humid basement, the angry whirr of the millstones under the hoppers, the high windows, powdered and darkened with the floating meal, the vague corners festooned with flour-laden cobwebs, the jolting and shaking of the bolting-cloths, had all a potentiality of terror in them that was not a pleasure to the boy's sensitive nerves. Ghosts, against all reason and experience, were but too probably waiting their chance to waylay unwary steps there whenever two feet ventured alone into the mill, and Indians, of course, made it their ambush.

With the sawmill it was another matter. That was always an affair of the broad day. It began work and quitted work like a Christian, and did not keep the gristmill's unnatural hours. Yet it had its fine moments, when the upright saw lunged through the heavy oak log and gave out the sweet smell of the bruised woody fibers, or then when the circular saw wailed through the length of the lath we were making for the new house, and freed itself with a sharp cry, and purred softly till the wood touched it again, and it broke again into its shrill lament. The warm sawdust in the pit below was almost as friendly to bare feet as the warm meal; and it was splendid to rush down the ways on the cars that brought up the logs or carried away the lumber.

It was in the early part of the second winter that it was justly thought fit I should leave these delights and go to earn some money in a printing-office in X——, when the foreman of the printing-office appeared one day at our cabin and asked if I could come to take the place of a delinquent hand. There was no question with any one but myself but I must go. For me, a terrible homesickness fell instantly upon me—a homesickness that already, in the mere prospect of absence, pierced my heart and filled my throat.

The foreman wanted me to go back with him in his buggy, but a day's grace was granted me, and then my elder brother took me to X——, where he was to meet my father at the railroad station on his return from Cincinnati. It had been snowing, in the soft Southern Ohio fashion, but the clouds had broken away, and the evening fell in a clear sky, apple-green along the horizon as we drove on. This color of the sky must always be associated for me with the despair which then filled my soul and which I was constantly swallowing down with great gulps. We joked, and got some miserable laughter out of the efforts of the horse to free himself from the snow that balled in his hoofs, but I suffered all the time an anguish of homesickness that now seems incredible. I had every fact of the cabin life before me; what each of the children was doing, especially the younger ones, and what, above all, my mother was doing, and how she was looking; and I saw the wretched little phantasm of myself moving about among them.

The editor to whom my brother delivered me over could
61

not conceive of me as tragedy; he received me as if I were the merest commonplace, and delivered me in turn to the good man with whom I was to board. There were half a dozen school-girls boarding there, too, and their gaiety, when they came in, added to my desolation. The man said supper was about ready, and he reckoned I would get something to eat if I looked out for myself. Upon reflection I answered that I thought I did not want any supper, and that I must go to find my brother, whom I had to tell something. I found him at the station and told him I was going home with him. He tried to reason with me, or rather with my frenzy of homesickness; and I agreed to leave the question open till my father came; but in my own mind it was closed.

My father suggested, however, something that had not occurred to either of us: we should both stay. This seemed possible for me; but not at that boarding-house, not within the sound of the laughter of those girls! We went to the hotel, where we had beefsteak and ham and eggs and hot biscuit every morning for breakfast, and where we paid two dollars apiece for the week we stayed. At the end of this time the editor had found another hand, and we went home, where I was welcomed as from a year's absence.

Again I was called to suffer a like trial, the chief trial of my boyhood, but it came in a milder form, and was lightened to me not only by the experience of survival from it, but by kindly circumstance. This time I went to Dayton, where my young uncle somehow learned the misery I was in, and bade me come and stay with him while I remained in the town. I was very fond of him, and of the gentle creature, his wife, but for all that, I was homesick still. I fell asleep with the radiant image of our log cabin before my eyes, and I woke with my heart like lead in my breast.

I did not see how I could get through the day, and I began it with miserable tears. I had found that by drinking a great deal of water at my meals I could keep down the sobs for the time being, and I practised this device to the surprise and alarm of my relatives, who were troubled at the spectacle of my unnatural thirst. But I could not wholly hide my suffering, and I suppose that after a while the sight of it became intolerable. At any rate, a blessed evening came when I returned from my work and found my brother waiting for me at my uncle's house; and the next morning we set out for home in the keen, silent dark before the November dawn.

We were both mounted on the italic-footed mare, I behind my brother, with my arms round him to keep on better; and so we rode out of the sleeping town, and into the lifting shadow of the woods. They might have swarmed with ghosts or Indians; I should not have cared; I was going home. By and by, as we rode on, the birds began to call one another from their dreams, the quails whistled from the stubble fields, and the crows clamored from the decaying tops of the girdled trees in the deadening; the squirrels raced along the fence-rails, and, in the woods, they stopped half-way up the boles to bark at us; the jays strutted down the shelving branches to offer us a passing insult and defiance.

Sometimes, at a little clearing, we came to a log cabin; the blue smoke curled from its chimney, and through the closed door came the low hum of a spinning-wheel. The red and yellow leaves, heavy with the cold dew, dripped round us; I was profoundly at peace, and the homesick will understand how it was that I was as if saved from death. At last we crossed the tail-race from the island, and turned up, not at the old log cabin, but at the front door of the new house. The family had flitted during my absence, and now they all burst out upon me in exultant welcome, and my mother caught me to her heart. Doubtless she knew that it would have been better for me to have conquered myself; but my defeat was dearer to her than my triumph could have been. She made me her honored guest; I had the best place at the table, the tenderest bit of steak, the richest cup of her golden coffee; and all that day I was "company."

It was a great day, which I must have spent chiefly in admiring the new house. It was so very new yet as not to be plastered; they had not been able to wait for that; but it was beautifully lathed in all its partitions, and the closely fitted floors were a marvel of carpentering. I roamed through the rooms, and up and down the stairs, and freshly admired the familiar outside of the house as if it were as novel as the interior, where open wood fires blazed upon the hearths and threw a pleasant light of home upon the latticed walls.

I must have gone through the old log cabin to see how it looked without us, but I have no recollection of ever entering its door again, so soon had it ceased to be part of my life. We remained in the new house, as we continued to call it, for two or three months, and then the changes of business which had been taking place without the knowledge of us children called us away from that roof, too, and we left the mills and the pleasant country that had grown so dear, to take up our abode in city streets again. We went to live in the ordinary brick house of our civilization, but we had grown so accustomed, with the quick and facile adaptation of children, to living in a house which was merely lathed, that we distinguished this last dwelling from the new house as a "plastered house."

Some of our playmates of the neighborhood walked part of the way to X—— with us boys, the snowy morning when we turned our backs on the new house to take

64

the train in that town. A shadow of the gloom in which our spirits were steeped passes over me again, but chiefly I remember our difficulties in getting our young New-foundland dog away with us; and our subsequent em-barrassments with him on the train, where he sat up and barked out of the window at the passing objects and finally became seasick, blot all other memories of that journey from my mind.

II

IF in a child's first years the things which it apparently remembers are really the suggestions of its elders, it begins soon to repay the debt, and repays it more and more fully until its memory touches the history of all whom it has known. Through the whole time when a boy is becoming a man his autobiography can scarcely be kept from becoming the record of his family and his world. He finds himself so constantly reflected in the personality of those about him, so blent with it, that any attempt to study himself as a separate personality is impossible. His environment has become his life, and his hope of a recognizable self-portrait must lie in his frank acceptance of the condition that he can make himself truly seen chiefly in what he remembers to have seen of his environment.

I

We were now going from the country to Columbus, where my father, after several vain attempts to find an opening elsewhere as editor or even as practical printer, had found congenial occupation at least for the winter; and the reader who likes to date a small event by a great one may care to know that we arrived in the capital of Ohio about the time that Louis Kossuth arrived in the capital of the United States. In the most impressive exile ever known he came from Hungary, then trampled under foot by the armies of Austria and Russia, and had been greeted with a frenzy of enthusiasm in New York as the prophet and envoy of a free republic in present difficulties, but destined to a glorious future. At Washington he had been received by both Houses of Congress with national honors which might well have seemed to him national promises of help against the despotisms joined in crushing the Magyar revolt; we had just passed a law providing for the arrest of slaves escaping from their owners in the South, and we were feeling free to encourage the cause of liberty throughout the world.

Kossuth easily deceived himself in us, and he went hopefully about the country, trying to float an issue of Hungarian bonds on our sympathetic tears, and in his wonderful English making appeals full of tact and eloquence, which went to the hearts if not the pockets of his hearers. Among the other state capitals he duly came to Columbus, where I heard him from the steps of the unfinished State House. I hung on the words of the picturesque black-bearded, black-haired, black-eyed man, in the braided coat of the Magyars, and the hat with an ostrich plume up the side which set a fashion among us, and I believed with all my soul that in a certain event we might find the despotisms of the Old World banded against us, and "would yet see Cossacks," as I thrilled to hear Kossuth say. In those days we world-patriots put the traitor Görgy, who surrendered the Hungarian army to the Austrians and Russians, beside our own Benedict Arnold; but what afterward became of him I do not know. I know that Kossuth went disappointed back to Europe and dwelt a more and more peaceful newspaper correspondent in Turin till the turn of fortune's wheel would have dropped him, somehow politically tolerable to Austria, back in his native country. But he would not return; he died in Turin; and a few years ago in Carlsbad I fancied I had caught sight of his son at a café, but was told that I had seen the wrong man, who was much more revolutionary-looking than Kossuth's son, and more like Kossuth.

I adopted with his cause the Kossuth hat, as we called it, and wore it with the plume in it till the opinions of boys without plumes in their hats caused me to take the feather out. My father was of their mind about the feather, but otherwise we thought a great deal alike, and he was zealous to have me see the wonders of the capital. I visited the penitentiary and the lunatic, deaf and dumb, and blind asylums with him, though I think rather from his interest than mine; but I was willing enough to realize the consequence of Columbus as the capital of a sovereign American state, and I did what I could to meet his expectations. Together we made as thorough examination of the new State House as the workmen who had not yet finished it would allow, and he told me that it would cost, when done, a million dollars, a sum of such immensity that my young imagination shrank from grappling with it; but I am afraid that before the State House was done it may have cost more; certainly it must have cost much more with the incongruous enlargements which in later years spoiled its classic proportions. My father made me observe that it was built of Ohio limestone without, and later I saw that it was faced with Vermont and Tennessee marble within, where it was not stuccoed and frescoed; but as for the halls of legislation where the laws of Ohio were made and provided, when I first witnessed the process, they were contained in a modest square edifice of brick which could not have cost a million dollars, or the twentieth part of them, by the boldest computation of the contractors. It was entirely modest as to the Hall of the House and the Senate Chamber, and I suppose that so were the state offices, wherever they were, unnoted by me. The State House, as much as I knew of it from a single visit to the Hall of Representatives, was of a very simple interior heated from two vast hearths where fires of cord-wood logs were blazing high. There were rows of legislators sitting at their desks, and probably one of them was on his feet, speaking; I recall dimly a presiding officer, but my main affair was to breathe as softly as I could and get away as soon as possible from my father's side where he sat reporting the proceedings for the *Ohio State Journal*, then the Whig and later the Republican organ.

II

Nobody cares now for the details, or even the main incidents of state legislation, but in that day people seemed to care so much that the newspapers at the capital found their account in following them, and as I learned later the papers at Cincinnati and Cleveland had correspondents at Columbus to let them know by letter what went on in the House and Senate. My father could make a very full and faithful report of the legislative proceedings in longhand, and for this he was paid ten dollars a week. As I have told elsewhere, I worked on the same paper and had four dollars as compositor; my eldest brother became very provisionally clerk in a grocery-store where he had three dollars, and read the novels of Captain Maryatt in the intervals of custom. Our joint income enabled us to live comfortably in the little brick house, on a humble new street, which my father hired for ten dollars a month from a Welsh carpenter with a large family. No sense of our own Welsh origin could render this family interesting; I memorized some scraps of their Cymric as I overheard it across the fence, but we American children did not make acquaintance with the small Welsh folk, or with more than these

69

few words of their language, which after several attempts at its grammar still remain my sole knowledge of it. On the other side lived a mild, dull German of some lowly employ, whom I remember for his asking us across the fence, one day, to lend him a leather cover. When by his patient repetition this construed itself as an envelope, we loved him for the pleasure it gave us, and at once made leather-cover the family name for envelope. Across the street dwelt an English family of such amiable intelligence that they admired some verses of mine which my father stole to their notice and which they put me to shame by praising before my face.

In my leisure from the printing-office I was in fact cultivating a sufficiently thankless muse in the imitation of Pope and Goldsmith, for in me, more than his other children, my father had divined and encouraged the love of poetry; but in reproducing his poets, as I constantly did, to his greater admiration than mine, I sometimes had a difficulty which I did not carry to him. There is no harm in now submitting it to the reader, who may have noted in his own case the serious disadvantage of writing about love when he had as yet had no experience of the passion. I did my best, and I suppose I did no worse than other poets of thirteen. But I fell back mostly upon inanimate nature, which I knew very well from the woods where I had hunted and the fields where I had hoed; to be honest, I never hoed so much as I hunted, and I never hunted very successfully. I now went many walks into the woods and fields about the town in my longing for the wider spaces I had known, and helped my sisters dig up the wild flowers which they brought home and planted in our yard. But I recall more distinctly than any other a Sunday walk which I took with my father across the Scioto to the forsaken town on the western bank of the river. Franklinton had been thought

70

of as the capital before Columbus, and it has now been rehabilitated in an indefinitely greater prosperity than it ever enjoyed in its prime, but during my life in the city which so promptly won the capital away from it, Franklinton lay abandoned by nine-tenths of its inhabitants, and stretched over the plain in rows of small, empty brick dwellings. I have the impression of disused county buildings, but I am not sure of them; I heard (but in days when I did not much concern myself with such poor unliterary facts) that the notion of Franklinton as the capital was rejected because it was apt in springtime to be flooded by the Scioto, and was at other seasons infested by malaria which the swarms of mosquitoes bore to every household. The people, mostly sallow women and children who still gaze at me from a few of the doorways and windows, looked as if their agues were of unfailing recurrence every other day of every week; though I suppose that in winter they were somewhat less punctual. I should like to believe that Franklinton was precious to me because of its suggestion of Goldsmith's *Deserted Village*, but I cannot claim that it bore any likeness to the hamlet of the poet's fancy, even in the day when I was hungering to resemble all life to literature; and I never made it the subject of my verse, though I think now it merited as much and more. Since that time I have seen other abandoned cities, notably Pompeii and Herculaneum, but Franklinton remains of a memorable pathos and of a forlornness all the more appreciable because it had become ruin and eld amidst the young, vigorous life of a new country.

In *My Literary Passions* I have made full mention of the books I was reading that winter of 1851–2; but I was rather surprised to find that in a boyish diary of the time, lately discovered in the chaos of a storage warehouse, none of my favorite authors was specified. I could trace them, indeed, in the varying style of the record, but the diarist seems to have been shy of naming them, for no reason that I can now imagine.

The diary is much more palpable than the emotions of the diarist, and is a large, flat volume of foolscap paper, bound in marbled boards, somewhat worn with use and stained with age. The paper within is ruled, which kept the diarist's hand from wandering, and the record fills somewhat less than a fourth of the pages; the rest are given to grammatical exercises in Spanish, which the diarist was presently beginning to study, but even these interrupt themselves, falter, and are finally lost in space. The volume looks quite its age of sixty years, for it begins in the closing months of 1851.

The diarist practised a different handwriting every day and wrote a style almost as varied. The script must have been imitated from the handwritings which he successively admired, and the literary manner from that which seemed to him most elegant in the authors he had latest read. He copies not only their style, but their mental poses, and is often sage beyond his years, which are fourteen verging upon fifteen. With all its variety of script, the spelling in the diary is uniformly of the correct sort which printers used to learn as part of their trade, but which is said to be now suffering a general decay through the use of typesetting machines. There are few grammatical errors in the diversified pages and the punctuation is accurate and intelligent.

Though there is little note or none of the diarist's reading, there is other witness that it had already begun to be of wide range and copious variety. Now and then there are hints of his familiarity with Goldsmith's Essays, and Dickens's novels which his father was reading aloud, and one Sunday it appears that when he was so loath to get up that he did not rise until eight o'clock he tells

72

us: "I slipped into my clothes, made the fire in the sitting-room, wrapped father's cloak about me, and sat down to read the travels of Hommaire de Hell, a Frenchman who traveled in the Russian Empire in the year 1840." I do not care much now who M. Hommaire de Hell was or what he had to say of the Russian Empire in 1840, but I wish I could see that boy wrapped in his father's cloak, and losing himself in the Frenchman's page. Though I have the feeling that we were once familiarly acquainted, I am afraid the diarist would not know me if he looked up across the space of threescore years, though he might divine in me a kindred sense of the heaviness of the long Sunday hours which he confronts when he rises from his reading.

Throughout the yellowing pages there is evident striving, not to say straining, for a literary style, the most literary style possible, and the very first page commemorates a visit to the Lunatic Asylum in terms of a noble participial construction. "Passing up the broad graveled path to the door of the institution, we entered the office, and leaving our hats on the table we proceeded on our way. The first room we entered contained those who were nearly cured. There was in it no one but an old and a young man. The old man I did not notice much, but the young one attracted my attention. He paced the floor all the time, not taking the least notice of us; then we went up-stairs where the most unmanageable ones were kept. Here was a motley crew, some of them lying at full length on the floor, standing up and walking about, while crownless hats and dilapidated shirt-bosoms were the order of the day. In the midst of these terrible men, thoughtless as the brute and ferocious as the tiger, stood a small man (the assistant physician) whom they could have torn limb from limb in a moment. Here was a beautiful instance of the power of mind over brute force.

He was reading poetry to them, and the men, totally bereft of reason, listening like little children to the sweet cadence of the verse." All this and more is in a fine script, so sloping that it is almost lying down, either from the exhausting emotions of the diarist or from a temporary ideal of elegance. But the very next day it braces itself for a new effort and it is not many days before it stands upright in a bold, vertical file.

The writer does not know any boys except in the printing-office, and these he knows only in a shrinking sort, not venturing to take part, except once, in their wild hilarity, and scarcely knowing their names, even the name of the boy whom he is afterward to associate himself with in their first venture with a volume of verse. His chief companionship is with his father, whom he goes long walks and holds long talks with, and it is his father who encourages him in his versifying and who presently steals into the print of the newspaper employing them both a poem on the premature warm weather which has invited the bluebirds and blackbirds into the northern March. At first the boy was in dismay at the sight of the poem, with the introductory editorial note customary in those days, but he hides this from his diary, where he confides his joy in finding his verses "copied into a New York paper, and also in the Cincinnati *Commercial*. I mean the piece on Winter."

But the poet kept on and wrote more and more, while the diarist wrote less and less. It is needless to follow him through the pieces which were mostly imitated from some favorite poet of the moment or more originally drawn from the scenes of life known to the author. One of these, painting an emigrant's farewell to the home he is leaving, tells how he stoops over—

> "And pats the good old house dog
> Who is lying on the floor."

The morning after the piece appeared, a fellow printer-boy seems to have quoted the line aloud for all to hear, and dramatized it by patting the author on the head, inwardly raging but helpless to resent the liberty. In fact, the poet did not well know how to manage the publicity now thrust upon him. He behaved indeed with such outrageous resentment at finding his first piece of verse in print that his father, who had smuggled it into the editor's hands, well-nigh renounced him and all his works. But not quite; he was too fond of both, and the boy and he were presently abetting each other in the endeavor for his poetic repute—so soon does the love of fame go to the strongest head.

As yet neither looked for his recognition in that sort of literature which the boy was ultimately to be best or most known in. He seems not to have read at this time much prose fiction, but he was reading Homer in Pope's translation, or rather he was reading the Odyssey; the Iliad he found tiresome and noisy; and if the whole truth must be told, as I have understood it, he liked *The Battle of the Frogs and Mice* best of all the Homeric poems. It was this which he imitated in a burlesque epic of *The Cat Fight*, studied from nature in the hostilities nightly raging on the back fences; but the only surviving poem of what may be called his classical period, as the poets of it understood Queen Anne's age, is a pastoral so exactly modeled upon the pastorals of the great Mr. Pope, that but for a faulty line here and there and the intrusion of a few live American birds among the stuffed songsters of those Augustan groves, I do not see how Mr. Pope could deny having written it. He might well have rejoiced in a follower who loved him so devotedly and so exactly reproduced his artificiality in heroic couplets studied from his own, with the same empty motive to the same unreal effect, as the surviving fragments of it will witness.

YEARS OF MY YOUTH

"When fair Aurora kissed the purple East
And dusky night the struggling day released,
Two swains whom Phœbus waked from sleep's embrace
Led forth their flocks to crop the dewy grass.
While morning blushed upon the cheek of day
Young Corydon began the rural lay.

Corydon.

"Now ceases Philomel her nightly strain,
    And trembling stars forsake the ethereal plain;
    Pale Luna fades and down the distant West
    Sadly and slowly lowers her rayless crest;
    But yellow Phœbus pours his beams along
    And linnets sport where Philomela sung.
    Here robins chirp and joyful orioles sing
    Where late the owlet flapped his noiseless wing;
    Here the pale lily spreads its petals wide,
    And snowy daisies deck the green hillside;
    Here violets' bloom with waterflowers wreath,
    And forest blossoms scent the Zephyr's breath.
    Fit spot for song where Spring in every flower
    Rich incense offers to the morning hour.
    Then let us sing! The hour is meet for love,
    The plain, the vale, the music-breathing grove;
    Let gentle Daphnis judge the doubtful song,
    And soft Æolus bear the notes along.
    I stake my pipe with whose soft notes I while
    The tedious hours, and my toil beguile;
    Whose mellow voice gives joy serener charms,
    And grief of half its bitterness disarms."

Here should enter some unnamed competitor, but apparently does not.

"And I, my dog, who guards by yonder brook
    Two careless truants from his master's flock;
    Who views his timid charge with jealous eyes
    And every danger for their sake defies.
    In cheerful day my helpmate and my pride,
    At night my brave companion and my guide.

76

The morning flies: no more the song delay,
　　For morning most delights the Sylvan Muse,
Ere modest twilight yields to flaming day,
　　And fervid sunbeams drink the cooling dews
And wither half the freshness of the Spring."

Another nameless person, possibly the "gentle Daphnis," now speaks:

"Alternate, then, ye swains must answering sing.
　　By turns the planets circle round the sun
In even turns the changing seasons run;
　　Smooth-coming night enshrouds the passing day,
And morn returning smiles the night away."

And doubtless now it is Corydon who resumes:

"Inspire my song, ye tuneful nine, inspire!
　　And fill the shepherd's humble lay with fire.
Around your altar verdant bays I twine,
　　And palms I offer on your sacred shrine.
Since Julia smiles, let Julia fire my strain,
　　And smooth the language of the lay of love
Till conscious music breathes o'er all the plain,
　　And joyous echoes wake the silent grove."

I have no facts to support my conjecture, but I will hazard the belief that the winter of 1851–2 was largely given to producing and polishing this plaster-of-paris masterpiece. I might find it easy to make a mock of the lifeless cast—a "cold pastoral," indeed!—but it would be with a faint, or perhaps more than faint, heartache for the boy who strove so fervently to realize a false ideal of beauty in his work. It is my consolation that his soul was always in his work and that when he turned to other ideals and truer, because faithfuler to the life he knew, he put his soul into them, too.

III

In the *State Journal* office I had soon been changed from the newspaper to the book room, and was put to setting up the House bills and Senate bills. I am not ready to say that these potential laws, with their clattering repetitions of, "An Act entitled an Act to amend an Act," intensified my sense of Columbus as a capital, with the lawmaking machinery always grinding away in it; but the formula had its fascination, and I remained contented with my work, with no apprehension, from the frequent half-holidays offered me by the foreman, that there was ever to be an end of it. All at once, however, the legislature had adjourned and my father's engagement ended with the session. My employment somehow ceased with both, and though we children were now no longer so home-sick for the country, and would have liked well enough to live on in Columbus, we were eager for the new home which he told us he had found for us in the Western Reserve. In his anti-slavery opinions he agreed better with the Ohio New-Englanders there than with the Ohio Virginians and Kentuckians whom we had hitherto lived amongst; we understood that he had got a share in the Freesoil newspaper in Ashtabula; and I can recall no wider interval between the adjournment of the legislature and our taking passage on the newly completed railroad to Cleveland than sufficed me for a hardy experiment in gardening among the obdurate clods and brickbats of our small back yard.

In the news-room of the *State Journal* office I had seen the first real poet of my personal knowledge in the figure of the young assistant editor who used to come in with proofs or copy for the foreman, but I cannot hope that the reader will recognize him in his true quality under the name of Florus B. Plympton, or will quite withhold the sophisticated smile of these days for the simple-hearted American parents of the past who could so christen an unconsenting infant. I dare say most of his verse was no worthier of his best than this name, but if here and there

a reader has known the lovely lines of the poem called
In Summer when the Days were Long, he will be glad to
have me recall it with him, and do what I can to bring
it back from dumb forgetfulness. I myself had not read
that poem when I used to see the young editor in the
news-room, and he had perhaps not yet written it; I believe I did not think any great things of other pieces which
he printed in the *State Journal;* and it was in the book-
room, where I was afterward transferred, that I all unwittingly met the truest poet of our Middle West, and one
of the truest poets of any time or place. With the name
of John J. Piatt I would gladly relate my own more
memorably than in the *Poems of Two Friends*, long since
promptly forgotten, where I joined him in our first literary
venture. We are now old men, hard upon our eighties,
but we were then boys of thirteen or fourteen, with no
dream of our adventure in joint-authorship, and we had
our boyish escapades in the long leisure of the spring
afternoons of 1850, when we did not yet know each other
even by the nature of poets which we shared.

I can see Piatt now, his blue eyes laughing to tears in
our romps and scuffles, and I can hear the trickling mirth of
his reluctant chuckle, distinct across the days of the years
that have brought us so far. He was setting up House
Bills and Senate Bills too, with whatever subjective effect,
in the intervals of our frolic, but his head must have been
involved in the sunny mists that wrapt mine round.
My life, then, as always, was full of literature to bursting,
the literature I read and the literature I wrote, for my
father had already printed some of the verses I could not
keep to myself; and it is not strange that I can recover
from the time so few and so trivial events of more exoteric
interest. My love indeed was primarily for my work at
the printer's case, but that had its hours, as while I was
distributing the type, when my fancy roamed the universe

in every dramatization of a proud and triumphant future. In these reveries I was a man brilliantly accepted by the great world, but in my waking from them I was a boy, with a boy's fears and anxieties in conditions which might not have appalled a bolder nature. There was, for instance, the Medical College in State Street, where years later I was to dwell so joyously when it had become a boarding-house in a suspense of its scientific function, but whence now, after the early dark had fallen, ghosts swarmed from the dissecting-room, and pursued me on my way home well round the corner into Oak Street, where they delivered me over to another peril, unfailingly in wait for me. There an abominable cur, which had instinctively known of my approach several houses away, rushed from his gate to meet me. It might have been my wisest course to run from the ghosts, but flight would not avail me with this little beast, and when he sprang out with sudden yelpings and barkings, and meteoric flashings about my legs, I was driven to the folly of trying to beat him off with sticks and stones. After he had once found his way to my terror, which remained to me from having been bitten by a dog years before, and left me without a formula of right behavior with a dog attacking me, nothing could save me from him but my final escape from his fence, his street, his city; and this, more than anything else, consoled me for any sense of loss which I may have felt in leaving the state capital.

IV

My elder brother and I had several ideals in common quite apart from my own literary ideals. One of these was life in a village, as differenced from life in the country, or in any city, large or little; another was the lasting renunciation of the printing-business in every form.

80

The last was an effect from the anxiety which we had shared with our father and mother in the long adversity, ending in the failure of his newspaper, from which we had escaped to the country. Once clear of that disaster, we meant never to see a press or a case of types again; and after our year of release from them in the country my brother had his hopes of learning the river and becoming a steamboat pilot, but failed in these, and so joined us in Columbus, where he had put off the evil day of his return to the printing-business a little longer. Meanwhile I had yielded to my fate and spent the whole winter in a printing-office; and now we were both going to take up our trade, so abhorrent in its memories, but going gladly because of the chances which it held out to my father at a time when there seemed no other chance in the world for him.

Yet we were about to fulfil our other ideal by going to live in a village. The paper which we were to help make my father make his by our work—for he had no money to buy it—was published in Ashtabula, now a rather obstreperous little city, full of industrial noise and grime, with a harbor emulous of the gigantic activities of the Cleveland lake-front, but it must even then have had a thousand people. Our ideal, therefore, was not perfectly realized till our office was transferred some ten miles inland to the county-seat, for whatever business and political reasons of the joint stock company which had now taken over the paper, with my father as editor. With its four hundred inhabitants less Jefferson was so much more than Ashtabula a village; and its young gaieties welcomed us and our little force of printers to a social liberty and equality which I long hoped some day to paint as a phase of American civilization worthy the most literal fidelity of fiction. But I shall now never do that, and I must be content to borrow from an earlier page some passages which uninventively record the real events and conditions of our enterprise.

In politics, the county was always overwhelmingly Freesoil, as the forerunner of the Republican party was then called; the Whigs had hardly gathered themselves together since the defeat of General Scott for the Presidency; the Democrats, though dominant in state and nation, and faithful to slavery at every election, did not greatly outnumber among us the zealots called Comeouters, who would not vote at all under a Constitution recognizing the right of men to own men. Our paper was Freesoil, and its field was large among that vast majority of the people who believed that slavery would finally perish if kept out of the territories and confined to the old Slave States.

The people of the county were mostly farmers, and of these nearly all were dairymen. The few manufactures were on a small scale, except perhaps the making of oars, which were shipped all over the world from the heart of the primeval forests densely wooding the vast levels of the region. The portable steam-sawmills dropped down on the borders of the woods have long since eaten their way through and through them, and devoured every stick of timber in most places, and drunk up the watercourses that the woods once kept full; but at that time half the land was in the shadow of those mighty poplars and hickories, elms and chestnuts, ashes and hemlocks; and the meadows that pastured the herds of red cattle were dotted with stumps as thick as harvest stubble. Now there are not even stumps; the woods are gone, and the watercourses are torrents in spring and beds of dry clay in summer. The meadows themselves have vanished, for it has been found that the strong yellow soil will produce more in grain than in milk. There is more money in the hands of the farmers there now, but half a century ago there was so much less that fifty dollars seldom passed through a farmer's hands in a year. Payment was made us in kind rather than in coin, and every sort of farm produce was legal tender at the printing-office. Wood was welcome in any quantity, for our huge box-stove consumed it with inappeasable voracity, and even then did not heat the wide, low room which was at once editorial-room, composing-room, and press-room. Perhaps this was not so much the fault of the stove as of the building. In that cold, lake-shore country the people dwelt in wooden structures almost as thin and flimsy as tents; and often in the first winter of our sojourn the type froze solid with the water which the compositor put on it when he wished to distribute his case, placed near the window so as to get all the light there was, but getting all the cold there was, too. From time to time the compositor's fingers became so stiff that blowing on them would not avail; he made many excursions between his stand and the stove; in severe weather he practised the device of warming his whole case of types by the fire, and, when they lost heat, warming it again.

The first floor of our office-building was used by a sash-and-blind factory; there was a machine-shop somewhere in it, and a mill for sawing out shingles; and it was better fitted to the exercise of these robust industries than to the requirements of our more delicate craft. Later, we had a more comfortable place, in a new wooden "business block," and for several years before I left it the office was domiciled in an old dwelling-house, which we bought, and which we used without much change. It could never have been a very comfortable dwelling, and my associations with it are of a wintry cold, scarcely less polar than that we were inured to elsewhere. In fact, the climate of that region is rough and fierce; I know that there were lovely summers and lovelier autumns in my time there, full of sunsets of a strange, wild, melancholy splendor, I suppose from some atmospheric influence of the lake; but I think chiefly of the winters, so awful to us after the mild seasons of southern Ohio; the frosts of ten and twenty below; the village streets and the country roads drowned in snow, the consumptives in the thin houses, and the "slippin'," as the sleighing was called, that lasted from December to April with hardly a break. At first our family was housed on a farm a little way out, because there was no tenement to be had in the village, and my father and I used to walk to and from the office together in the morning and evening. I had taught myself to read Spanish, in my passion for *Don Quixote*, and I was now, at the age of fifteen, intending to write a life of Cervantes. The scheme occupied me a good deal in those bleak walks, and perhaps it was because my head was so hot with it that my feet were always very cold; but my father assured me that they would get warm as soon as my boots froze. If I have never yet written that life of Cervantes, on the other hand I have never been quite able to make it clear to myself why my feet should have got warm when my boots froze.

v

It may have been only a theory of his; it may have been a joke. He had a great many theories and a great many jokes, and together they always kept life interesting and sunshiny for him. With his serene temperament and his happy doubt of disaster in any form, he was singularly fitted to encounter the hardships of a country editor's lot. But for the moment, and for what now seems a long time after the removal of our paper to the county-seat, these seem to have vanished. The printing-office was the center of civic and social interest; it was frequented by visitors at all times, and on publication day it was a scene of gaiety that looks a little incredible in the retrospect. The place was as bare and rude as a printing-office seems always to be: the walls were splotched with ink and the floor littered with refuse newspapers; but, lured by the novelty of the affair, and perhaps attracted by a natural curiosity to see what manner of strange men the printers were, the school-girls and young ladies of the village flocked in and made it like a scene of comic opera, with their pretty dresses and faces, their eager chatter and lively energy in folding the papers and addressing them to the subscribers, while our fellow-citizens of the place, like the bassos and barytones and tenors of the chorus, stood about and looked on with faintly sarcastic faces. It would not do to think now of what sorrow life and death have since wrought for all those happy young creatures, but I may recall without too much pathos the sensation when some citizen volunteer relaxed from his gravity far enough to relieve the regular mercenary at the crank of our huge power-press wheel, amid the applause of the whole company.

We were very vain of that press, which replaced the hand-press hitherto employed in printing the paper. This was of the style and make of the hand-press which superseded the Ramage press of Franklin's time; but it had been decided to signalize our new departure by the purchase of a power-press of modern contrivance and of a speed fitted to meet the demands of a sub-scription-list which might be indefinitely extended. A deputation of the leading politicians accompanied the editor to New York, where he went to choose the machine, and where he bought a second-hand Adams press of the earliest pattern and patent. I do not know, or at this date I would not undertake to say, just what principle governed his selection of this superannuated veteran; it seems not to have been very cheap; but possibly he had a prescience of the disabilities which were to task his ingenuity to the very last days of that press. Certainly no man of less gift and skill could have coped with its infirmities, and I am sure that he thoroughly enjoyed nursing it into such activity as carried it hysterically through those far-off publication days. It had obscure functional disorders of various kinds, so that it would from time to time cease to act, and would have to be doctored by the hour before it would go on. There was probably some organic trouble, too, for, though it did not really fall to pieces on our hands, it showed itself incapable of profiting by several improvements which he invented, and could, no doubt, have successfully applied to the press if its constitution had not been undermined. It went with a crank set in a prodigious fly-wheel which revolved at a great rate, till it came to the moment of making the impression, when the whole mechanism was seized with such a reluctance as nothing but an heroic effort at the crank could overcome. It finally made so great a draught upon our forces that it was decided to substitute steam for muscle in its operation, and we got a small engine which could fully sympathize with the press in having seen better days. I do not know that there was anything the matter with the engine itself, but the boiler had some peculiarities which might well mystify the casual spectator. He could easily have satisfied himself that there was no danger of its blowing up when he saw my brother feeding bran or cornmeal into its safety-valve in order to fill up certain seams or fissures in it which caused it to give out at the moments of the greatest reluctance in the press. But still he must have had his misgivings of latent danger of some other kind, though nothing ever actually happened of a hurtful character. To this day I do not know just where

86

those seams or fissures were, but I think they were in the boiler-head, and that it was therefore suffering from a kind of chronic fracture of the skull. What is certain is that, somehow, the engine and the press did always get us through publication day, and not only with safety, but often with credit; so that many years after, when I was at home, and my brother and I were looking over an old file of the paper, we found it much better printed than either of us expected; as well printed, in fact, as if it had been done on an old hand-press, instead of the steam-power press which it vaunted the use of. The wonder was that, under all the disadvantages, the paper was ever printed on our steam-power press at all; it was little short of miraculous that it was legibly printed, and altogether unaccountable that such impressions as we found in that file could come from it. Of course, they were not average impressions; they were the very best out of the whole edition, and were as creditable as the editorial make-up of the sheet.

VI

Upon the whole, our paper was an attempt at conscientious and self-respecting journalism; it addressed itself seriously to the minds of its readers; it sought to form their tastes and opinions. I do not know how much it influenced them, if it influenced them at all, and as to any effect beyond the circle of its subscribers, that cannot be imagined, even in a fond retrospect. But since no good effort is altogether lost, I am sure that this endeavor must have had some tacit effect; and I am sure that no one got harm from a sincerity of conviction that devoted itself to the highest interests of the reader, that appealed to nothing base, and flattered nothing foolish in him. It went from our home to the homes of the people in a very literal sense, for my father usually brought his exchanges from the office at the end of his day there, and made his selections or wrote his editorials while the household work went on him, about and his children gathered around the same lamp, with their books or their jokes; there were a good many of both.

Our county was the most characteristic of that remarkable group of counties in northern Ohio called the Western Reserve, and forty years ago the population was almost purely New England in origin, either by direct settlement from Connecticut, or indirectly after the sojourn of a generation in New York State. We were ourselves from southern Ohio, where the life was then strongly tinged by the adjoining life of Kentucky and Virginia, and we found these transplanted Yankees cold and blunt in their manners; but we did not undervalue their virtues. They were very radical in every way, and hospitable to novelty of all kinds. I imagine that they tested more new religions and new patents than have been even heard of in less inquiring communities. When we came among them they had lately been swept by the fires of spiritualism, which left behind a great deal of smoke and ashes where the inherited New England orthodoxy had been. They were temperate, hard-working, hard-thinking folks, who dwelt on their scattered farms, and came up to the county fair once a year, when they were apt to visit the printing-office and pay for their papers. They thought it droll, as people of the simpler occupations are apt to think all the more complex arts; and one of them once went so far in expression of his humorous conception as to say, after a long stare at one of the compositors dodging and pecking at the type in his case, "Like an old hen pickin' up millet." This sort of silence, and this sort of comment, both exasperated the printers, who took their revenge as they could. They fed it full, once, when a country subscriber's horse, hitched

88

before the office, crossed his hind legs and sat down in his harness like a tired man, and they proposed to go out and offer him a chair, to take him a glass of water, and ask him to come inside. Fate did not often give them such innings; they mostly had to create their chances of reprisal, but they did not mind that.

There was always a good deal of talk going on, but, although we were very ardent politicians, our talk was not political. When it was not mere banter, it was mostly literary; we disputed about authors among ourselves and with the village wits who dropped in, and liked to stand with their backs to our stove and challenge opinion concerning Holmes and Poe, Irving and Macaulay, Pope and Byron, Dickens and Shakespeare. But it was Shakespeare who was oftenest on our tongues; indeed, the printing-office of former days had so much affinity with the theater that compositors and comedians were almost convertible. Religion entered a good deal into our discussions, which my father, the most tolerant of men, would not suffer to become irreverant. Part of his duty, as publisher of the paper, was to bear patiently with the type of farmer who thought he wished to discontinue his paper, and really wished to be talked into continuing it. I think he rather enjoyed letting such a subscriber talk himself out, and carrying him from point to point in his argument, always consenting that he knew best what he wanted to do, but skilfully persuading him at last that a home paper was more suited to his needs than any city substitute. Once I could have given the heads of his reasoning, but they are gone from me now.

He was like all country editors then, and I dare say now, in being a printer as well as an editor, and he took a just share in the mechanical labors. These were formerly much more burdensome, for twice or thrice the present type-setting was then done in the country offices.

In that time we had three journeymen at work and two or three girl-compositors, and commonly a boy-apprentice besides. The paper was richer in a personal quality, and the printing-office was unquestionably more of a school. After we began to take girl-apprentices it became coeducative, as far as they cared to profit by it; but I think it did not serve to widen their thoughts or quicken their wits as it did those of the boys. They looked to their craft as a living, not as a life, and they had no pride in it. They did not learn the whole trade, as the journeymen had done; but served only such apprenticeship as fitted them to set type; and their earnings were usually as great at the end of a month as at the end of a year.

VII

The printing-office had been my school from childhood so largely that I could almost say I had no other, but the time had come, even before this, when its opportunities did not satisfy the hunger which was always in me for knowledge convertible into such beauty as I imagined and wished to devote my life to. I was willing and glad to do my part in helping my father, but he recognized my right to help myself forward in the line of my own longing, and it was early arranged that I should have a certain measure of work to do, and when it was done I should be free for the day. My task was finished early in the afternoon, and then my consuming pleasures began when I had already done a man's work. I was studying four or five languages, blindly and blunderingly enough, but with a confidence at which I can even now hardly smile; I was attempting many things in verse and prose which I seldom carried to a definite close, and I was reading, reading, reading, right and left, hither and yon, wherever an author tempted me. I was not

meaning to do less than the greatest things, or to know
less than the most, but my criticism outran my performance and exacted of me an endeavor for the perfection
which I found forever beyond me. Far into the night
I clung to my labored failures in rhyme while I listened
for the ticking of the death-watch in the walls of my little
study; or if I had imagined, in my imitations of others'
fiction, some character that the poet had devoted to an
early death, I helplessly identified myself with that character, and expected his fate. It was the day when this
world was much more intimate with the other world
than it is now, and the spiritualism which had evoked its
phenomena through most houses in the village had left
them haunted by dread sounds, if not sights; but it
was not yet the day when nervous prostration had got
its name or was known in its nature. For me this malady
came in the hypochondria which was misery not less
real because at the end of the ends I knew it to be the
exaggeration of an apprehension without ground in
reality.

I have hesitated to make any record of this episode,
but I think it essential to the study of my very morbid
boyhood, and I hope some knowledge of it may be help-
ful to others in like suffering. Somehow as a child I
had always had a terror of hydrophobia, perhaps from
hearing talk of that poor man who had died of it in the
town where we then lived, and when years afterward I
was, as I have told, bitten by a dog, my terror was the
greater because I happened to find myself alone in the
house when I ran home. I had heard of excising a snake-
bite to keep the venom from spreading, and I would now
have cut out the place with my knife, if I had known
how. In the end I did nothing, and when my father
came home he did not have the wound cauterized. He
may have believed that anything which tended to fix my

91

mind upon it would be bad, and perhaps I forgot it the sooner for his decision. I have not forgotten the make of the gloomy autumnal afternoon when the thing happened, or the moment when years afterward certain unguarded words awoke the fear in me which as many more years were needed to allay. By some chance there was talk with our village doctor about hydrophobia, and the capricious way the poison of a dog's bite may work. "Works round in your system," he said, "for seven years or more, and then it breaks out and kills you." The words he let heedlessly fall fell into a mind prepared by ill-health for their deadly potency, and when the summer heat came I was helpless under it. Somehow I knew what the symptoms of the malady were, and I began to force it upon myself by watching for them. The splash of water anywhere was a sound I had to set my teeth against, lest the dreaded spasms should seize me; my fancy turned the scent of the forest fires burning round the village into the subjective odor of smoke which stifles the victim. I had no release from my obsession, except in the dreamless sleep which I fell into exhausted at night, or that little instant of waking in the morning, when I had not yet had time to gather my terrors about me, or to begin the frenzied stress of my effort to experience the thing I dreaded. There was no longer question of work for me, with hand or head. I could read, yes, but with the double consciousness in which my fear haunted every line and word without barring the sense from my perception. I read many novels, where the strong plot befriended me and formed a partial refuge, but I did not attempt escape in the poor boyish inventions, verse or prose, which I had fondly trusted might be literature. Instinct taught me that some sort of bodily fatigue was my safety; I spent the horrible days in the woods with a gun, or in the fields

92

gathering wild berries, and walked to and from the distant places that I might tire myself the more. My father reasoned to the same effect for me, and helped me as best he could; of course I was released from my tasks in the printing-office, and he took me with him in driving about the country on political and business errands. We could not have spent many days in this way, when, as it seems, I woke one morning in a sort of crisis, and having put my fear to the test of water suddenly dashed from a doorway beside me and failed of the convulsion which I was always expecting, I began imperceptibly to get the better of my demon. My father's talk always distracted me somewhat, and that morning especially his disgust with the beefsteak fried in lard which the landlady gave us for breakfast at the country tavern where we had passed the night must even have amused me, as a touch of the comedy blent with the tragedy in the Shakespearian drama of life. But no doubt a more real help was his recurrence, as often as I chose, to his own youthful suffering from hypochondria, and his constantly repeated assurance that I not only would not and could not have hydrophobia from that out-dated dog-bite, but that I must also soon cease to have hypochondria. I understood as well as he that it was not the fear of that malady which I was suffering, but the fear of the fear; that I was in no hallucination, no illusion as to the facts, but was helpless in the nervous prostration which science, or our poor village medicine, was yet many years from knowing or imagining. I have heard and read that sometimes people in their apprehension of the reality can bring on a false hydrophobia and die of it in the agonies their fancy creates. It may be so; but all that fear could do was done in me; and I did not die.

I could not absolutely fix the moment when I began to find my way out of the cloud of misery which lowered on my life, but I think that it was when I had gathered a little strength in my forced respite from work, and from the passing of the summer heat. It was as if the frost which people used to think put an end to the poisonous miasm of the swamps, but really only killed the insect sources of the malaria, had wrought a like sanitation in my fancy. My fear when it once lifted never quite overwhelmed me again, but it was years before I could endure the sight of the word which embodied it; I shut the book or threw from me the paper where I found it in print; and even now, after sixty years, I cannot bring myself to write it or speak it without some such shutting of the heart as I knew at the sight or sound of it in that dreadful time. The effect went deeper than I could say without accusing myself of exaggeration for both good and evil. In self-defense I learnt to practise a psychological juggle; I came to deal with my own state of mind as another would deal with it, and to combat my fears as if they were alien.

I cannot leave this confession without the further confession that though I am always openly afraid of dogs, secretly I am always fond of them; and it is only fair to add that they reciprocate my liking with even exaggerated affection. Dogs, especially of any more ferocious type, make up to me in spite of my diffidence; and at a hotel where we were once passing the summer the landlord's bulldog, ugliest and dreadest of his tribe, used to divine my intention of a drive and climb into my buggy, where he couched himself on my feet, with a confidence in my reciprocal tenderness which I was anxious not to dispel by the least movement.

VIII

As soon as my nerves regained something of their former tone, I renewed my struggle with those alien languages, using such weapons as I could fit my hand to. Notably there was a most comprehensive manual which, because it proposed instruction in so many languages, I called (from my father's invention or my own, for I had early learnt the trick of his drolling) a sixteen-bladed grammar. I wish now I could see that book, which did not include Greek or Hebrew or German, but abounded in examples of Latin, Italian, French, Spanish and probably Portuguese, and other tongues of that kinship, with literal versions of the texts. These versions falsified the native order of the words to the end that the English of them might proceed in the wonted way, and when I detected the imposition, I was the more offended because the right order of the words in those idioms was always perplexing me. The sixteen-bladed grammar was superseded by the ordinary school-books, Arnold's for Latin, and Anthon's for Greek, but the perplexities of one sort or other persisted. Such a very little instruction would have enlightened me; but who was to give it me? My father, perhaps, but he may not have known how, though in his own youth he had written an English grammar and more or less taught it, or he may have thought I would find it out for myself. He would have temperamentally trusted to that; he was always prouder than I of what I did unaided; he believed I could do everything without help. That was an error, but more than I ever could say do I owe to his taste in literature and the constant guidance up to a certain limit which he gave me. When I came back from the fields and woods with the sense of their beauty, and eager to turn it into literature, he guarded me against translating it in the terms of my English poets, with their larks and nightingales, their daisies and cowslips. He contended that our own birds and flowers were quite as good, besides being genuine; but he taught me to love the earlier English classics; and if I began to love the later classics, both English and American, and to be his guide in turn, this is only saying that each one is born of his generation. The time came early in our companionship when he thought fit to tell me that he regarded me as different from other boys of my age; and I had a very great and sweet happiness without alloy of vanity, from his serious and considered words. He did not say that he expected great things of me; though I had to check his fondness in offering my poor endeavors for the recognition of print, and I soon had the support of editors in this. But he justified himself and convinced me by once bringing to our house a kindly editor from a neighboring city whom he showed some of my things, and who carried away with him one of the minutely realistic sketches in which I had begun to practise such art as I have been able to carry farthest. When week after week the handsomely printed *Ohio Farmer* came with something in it, verse or prose, which I had done, I am not sure I had greater joy in it than my father, though now he thought it well to hide his joy as I always did mine.

All the while I was doing sketches and studies and poems for our own paper, which I put into type without first writing them, and short stories imitated from some favorite author of the moment with an art which I imagined must conceal itself from the reader. Once I carried Shakespeare beyond himself in a scene transferred from one of the histories, with such comedy characters as Pistol and Bardolph speaking the interchangeable prose and verse of his plays in adapting themselves to some local theme, which met with applause from the group of middle-aged cronies whom I most consorted with at the time. Once, also, I attempted a serial romance which, after a succession of several numbers, faltered and at last would not go on. I have told in another place how I had to force it to a tragic close without mercy for the heroine, hurried to an untimely death as the only means of getting her out of the way, and I will not repeat the miserable details here. It was a thing which could not meet with praise from any one, not even my father, though he did his best to comfort me in the strange disaster.

If my mother was the heart, he was the soul of our family life. In those young days when he did so much of his newspaper work at home he would always turn from it to take part in our evening jollity. He was gladly our equal in the jokes which followed around our table; and when he was stricken in his great age with the paralysis which he rallied from for a time, it was his joy to join his gray-haired children at the board in his wheeled chair and share in their laughing and making laugh. It seems to me that I can render him intelligible by saying that while my very religious-minded grandfather expected and humbly if fervently hoped to reach a heaven beyond this world by means of prayers and hymns and revivals and conversions, my not less religious-minded father lived for a heaven on earth in his beloved and loving home; a heaven of poetry and humor, and good-will and right thinking. He made it that sort of heaven for himself, and as he was the bravest man I have known because he never believed there was any danger, I think he must have felt himself as safe from sorrow in it as if he were in the world beyond this. When one of my younger brothers died, he was as if astonished that such a thing could be; it burst his innocent and beautiful dream; and afterward when I first met him, I was aware of his clinging, a broken man, to what was left of it. Death struck again and again, and he shrank under the bewildering blows; but a sense of that inexpressible pathos of his first bereavement remains with me.

IX

The family scene that passed in that earlier time was not always as idyllic as I have painted it. With five brothers in it there was often the strife which is always openly or covertly between brothers. My elder brother, who was four years my elder, had changed from the whimsical tease and guardian angel of our childhood to the anxious taskmaster of our later boyhood, requiring the same devotion in our common work that his conscience exacted of himself. I must say that for my own part I labored as faithfully as he, and I hotly resented his pressure. Hard words passed between us two, as blows, not very hard, had passed, while we were still children, between me and my younger brothers. But however light the blows were, they had to be disclaimed, and formal regret expressed, at my father's insistence. He would ascertain who struck the first blow, and when he had pronounced that wrong he would ask, "And you struck him back?" If the fact could not be denied, he went on to the further question, "Well, do two wrongs make a right?" Clearly they did not, and nothing remained but reluctant apology and reconciliation. Reason and civic morality were on his side, but I could not feel that justice was, and it seems to me yet that the primary offender was guiltier than the secondary.

Long ago, long before our youth was passed, utter forgiveness passed between my elder brother and me. The years since were years of such mutual affection as I could not exaggerate the sense of in tenderness and constancy, and the exchange of trust and honor. He came even in our youth to understand my aim in life, and feel what was always leading me on. He could not understand, perhaps, why poetry in literature should be so all in all with me, but he felt it in nature as keenly and deeply as I; and I have present now the experience of driving with him one September afternoon (on some chase of the delinquent subscriber), when he owned by his few spare words the unity of the beautiful in everything as I spoke the melting lines of Tennyson:

> "Tears, idle tears, I know not what they mean.
> Tears from the depths of some divine despair
> Rise in the heart and gather to the eyes,
> In looking on the happy autumn-fields,
> And thinking of the days that are no more."

He had a grotesque humor which vented itself in jokes at the expense of my mother's implicit faith in everything he said, as when she wondered how the cow got into the garden, and he explained, "She pulled out the peg with her teeth and put it under her fore leg and just walked through the gate," and my mother answered, "Well, indeed, indeed, I believe she did, child." She had little humor of her own, but she had a childlike happiness in the humor of us others, though she would not suffer joking from any but him. She relied upon him in everything, but in some things she drew a sharp line between the duties of her boys and girls in the tradition of her Pennsylvania origin. Indoor work was for girls, and outdoor for boys, and we shared her slight for the Yankee men who went by our gate to the pasture with their milk-pails. That was woman's work though it was outdoor work; and though it was outdoor work to kill chickens for the table, none of us boys had the heart to cut their heads off because we could not bear to witness their post-mortem struggles; but my brother brought out his gun and shot them, and this pursuit of them as game in our barnyard got us over a difficulty otherwise insuperable. The solution of our scruple, which my father shared, must have amused him; but my brother took it seriously. His type of humor was in the praise which long afterward he gave a certain passage of my realistic fiction, when he said it was as natural as the toothache.

Throughout that earlier time my father's chief concern was first that very practical affair of making his paper pay for the office and the house, and then incidentally preventing the spread of slavery into the territories. He was willing enough, I fancy, to yield his silent partnership in my studies to the young printer who now, for no reason that I can remember, began to take an active share in them. I have told in *My Literary Passions* how J. W. and I read Cervantes and Shakespeare together; but I could not say just why or when we began to be boon companions in our self-conducted inquiries into Latin and Greek, and then into German, which presently replaced Spanish in my affections through the witchery of Heine. He had the definite purpose of making those languages help him to a professorship in a Western college, but if I had any clear purpose it was to possess myself of their literature. To know them except to read them I do not think I cared; I did not try to speak or write the modern tongues; to this day I could not frame a proper letter in Spanish, German, French, or Italian, but I have a literary sense of them all. I wished to taste the fruit of my study before I had climbed the tree where it grew, and in a manner I did begin to gather the fruit without the interposition of the tree. Without clear knowledge of their grammatical forms, I imitated their literary forms. I cast my poetry, such as it was, into the metres of the Spanish poets I was reading, and without instruction or direction I acquainted myself with much of their literary history. I once even knew from the archaic tragedy of her name who Iñez de Castro was; I do not know now.

My friendship with J. W. early became chief of the many friends of a life rich in friendships. He was like most of his craft in his eccentric comings and goings to and from our employ, when sometimes we had no work to give him, and sometimes he had none to give us. When he left us he always went to Wisconsin, where he had once lived; and when he came back from one of these absences he would bring with him bits of character which he gave for our joy in his quaint observance, such as that of the mother who complained of her daughter because "she didn't cultivate her featur's none; she just let 'em hing and wallop," or the school-mistress who genteelly explained in the blackberry-patch where he found her, that she was "just out picking a few berries for tea-he-he-he," or the country bachelor who belatedly made up his mind to marry, and in his default of female acquaintance took his place on the top rail of a roadside fence, and called to the first woman who passed, "Say! You a married woman?" and then at the frightened answer, indignantly gasped out, "Yes, sir!" offered a mere "Oh!" for all apology and explanation, and let himself vanish by falling into the corn-field behind him.

J. W. literally made his home with us, for as if the burden of work for our own large family were not enough for my mother, we had always some of the printers, men or maids, to board. He entered into the spirit of our life; but it was recognized that he was peculiarly my friend, and we were left to our special comradeship. In that village nearly everybody played or sang, and in the summer nights the young people went about serenading one another's houses, under the moon which was then always full; and J. W. shared in every serenade where a tenor voice was welcome. At the printing-office, in the afternoon when the compositors were distributing their cases, he led the apprentice-girls in the songs which once filled the whole young world. The songs were often poverty-stricken enough in sentiment, and I suppose cheap and vulgar in music, but they were better than the silence that I should once have said had followed them. Yet only last winter in a hotel on the New Jersey coast, where there was some repairing in the corridor outside my room, the young painters and carpenters gathered at their lunch near my door, and after they had begun to joke they suddenly began to sing together as if it were still the habit for people of their lot to do so, in a world I had thought so hushed, except for its gramaphones; and though I could not make out the words, the gentle music somehow saved them from seeming common. It went to my heart, and made me glad of life where youth still sang as it used to sing when I was young.

Sometimes the village serenaders came to me, and then I left my books and stumbled down to the gate, half dazed, to find the faces I knew before they flashed away with gay shrieking and shouting; and J. W. among them, momentarily estranged from me, jealous in that world where we had our intimacy. My ambition was my barrier from the living world around me; I could not beat my way from it into that; it kept me absent and hampered me in the vain effort to be part of the reality I have always tried to portray. Though J. W. expected to make a more definite use of our studies, he seemed to understand me as well at least as I understood myself in my vaguer striving. I do not now remember reading him the things I was trying to write; or of his speaking to me of them. Perhaps my shyness, my pride, went so far as keeping them from him, though I kept from him so few of my vagaries in that region of hopes and fears where youth chiefly has its being.

102

The songs he had were as many as the stories, but there was one song, often on the tongues of the village serenaders, which was oftenest on his, and which echoes to me still from those serenades and those choral afternoons in the printing-office, and more distinctly yet from what we felt a midnight of wild adventure, when he sang it alone. We had gone to call together on two of our village girls at school fifteen miles away, and had set out in the flattering temperature of a January thaw; but when we started home, many hours into the dark, the wind had whipped round from the south to the north and had frozen the curdling slush into icy ruts under the runners of our sleigh. Our coats were such as had suited the thaw, but J. W. had a pair of thin cotton gloves for driving, while I had none. We took turns in driving at first, but as the way lengthened the cold strengthened and I cowered definitively under our buffalo robe, then the universal provision against the rigor of winter travel. For a while we shouted together in some drama of the situation, but by and by our fun froze at our lips, and then J. W. began to sing that song he used oftenest to sing:

> "Talk not to me of future bliss,
> Talk not to me of joys gone by!
> The happiest time is this!"

He kept the measure of the tune by beating on the robe above my head, first with one fist and then the other, as he passed the reins from hand to hand, and by pounding with both feet on the floor of the sleigh beside me. We lived through the suffering of that drive partly because he was twenty-two years old and I was eighteen, but partly also because we realized the irony of the song, with all the joke of it. Yet it was a long nightmare of misery, with a moment of supreme anguish, when we stopped at the last toll-gate, two miles from home, and the keeper came shuddering out with his red blot of a lantern. Then the song stopped for an instant, but seems to have begun again, and not ended till we sat with our feet in the oven of the kitchen stove at home, counting our adventure all gain. The memory of it brings before me again the face of my friend, with its beautiful regularity of feature, its pale blue eyes, its smooth, rich, girlish complexion, and its challenging, somewhat mocking smile. But the date when I saw him last in life is lost to me. He went to Wisconsin, as usual, but there was no wonted return; we kept each other present in the long letters which we wrote so long, but they faltered with time and ceased, and I can only make sure now that he got the professorship he aimed at in some seat of learning so modest that it has kept its name from me; and then, years after, that he went into the war for the Union and was killed.

X

I had now begun to be impatient of the village, and when it came to my last parting with J. W., which I did not know was the last, I felt the life very dull and narrow which I had once found so vivid and ample. There had come the radiant revelation of girlhood, and I had dwelt in the incredible paradise where we paired or were paired off each with some girl of his fancy or fancied fancy. There had been the ranging of the woods in autumn for chestnuts and in the spring for wintergreen; there had been the sleigh-rides to the other villages and the neighboring farms where there was young life waiting to welcome us through the drifting snows; there had been the dances at the taverns and the parties at the girls' houses with the games and the frolics, and the going home each with the chosen one at midnight and the long lingering at the gate: there had been the moonlight walks; there had

104

been the debating societies and the spelling-matches; there had been the days of the County Fair and the Fourths-of-July, and the Christmases rehabilitated from Dickens; and there had been the impassioned interest of the easily guessed anonymous letters of St. Valentine's day. But these things had passed, and with a certain disappointment suffered and yet prized there had come the sense of spent witchery and a spell outworn, and I chose to revolt from it all and to pine for a wider world and prouder pleasures. Distance in time and space afterward duly set the village I had wearied of in a truer and kinder light, and I came to value it as the potential stuff of such fiction as has never yet been written, and now never will be by me. I came to see that it abounded in characteristics and interests which differenced it from any other village, and I still think the companionship to which I passed in the absences of J. W. such as would make into the setting for as strange a story as we could ask of reality in the days when we wished life to surpass romance in strangeness.

I have told in *My Literary Passions* of the misanthropical Englishman who led in our Dickens-worship and played the organ in the little Episcopal church, and built the organs for such country churches about as could afford to replace their moaning melodions with them. I have said, I hope without too much attempt to establish the fact, that he was also a house-painter, and that in the long leisures of our summer days and winter nights and in the throes of his perpetual dyspepsia he was the inveterate antagonist in argument of the vivid Yankee who built steam-engines among us, and had taught school, and turned his quick head and hand to any art or trade which making an easy living exacted of him. They both lavishly lent me their books, and admitted me on equal terms to their intellectual enmity and amity, which was shared in some tacit way with a clever New England trader in watches, clocks, and jewelry. He came and went among us on visits more or less prolonged from some Eastern center of his commerce (my memory somehow specifies Springfield, Massachusetts), and he had a shrewd smile and kindly twinkling eye which represent him to me yet. He seldom took part in the disputes nightly held at the drug-and-book store; but not from want of spirit, when he had the boldness to deny some ferocious opinion exploded by the organ-builder in an access of indigestion.

The disputes nearly always involved question of the existence of a God, which was thought improbable by both of the debaters, and the immortality of the soul, which was doubted, in spite of the spiritualism rife in every second house in the village, with manifestations by rappings, table-tippings, and oral and written messages from another world through psychics of either sex, but oftenest the young girls one met in the dances and sleigh-rides. The community was prevalently unreligious; there was an ageing attendance at the Baptist and Methodist churches, but there was no stated service of the Congregationalists, though there was occasional preaching at their house and sometimes a lecture from an anti-slavery apostle, who wasted his doctrine on a community steeped in it already. Among many of the young people of the village the prevalent tone was irreverent to mocking in matters of religion; but their unlimited social freedom was without blame and without scandal, and if our villagers were not religious, they were, in a degree which I still think extraordinary, literary. Old and young they read and talked about books, and better books than people read and talk about now, as it seems to me, possibly because there were not so many bad ones; the English serials pirated into our magazines were followed and discussed, and any American author who made an effect in the East became promptly known in that small village of the Western Reserve. There were lawyers, of those abounding at every county-seat, who were fond of reading, and imparted their taste to the young men studying law in their offices. I might exaggerate the fact, but I do not think I have done so, or that I was much deceived as to a condition which reported itself, especially to me whose whole life was in books, through the sympathy I met in the village houses. I was always reading whatever came to hand, either with an instinct for what was good in my choice of books or with good fortune in my chance of them. Literature was so commonly accepted as a real interest, that I do not think I was accounted altogether queer in my devotion to it. To be sure, at an evening session in one of the dry-goods and grocery stores where question of me came up, it was decided that I would be nowhere in a horse-trade, but this was a rare instance of slight, and I do not believe that my disability would have been generally counted against me.

XI

Somewhere about this time I gave a month to the study of law in the office of the United States Senator dwelling among us. I have never regretted reading a first volume of Blackstone through, or not going on to the second; his frank declaration that the law was a jealous mistress and would brook no divided love, was upon reflection quite enough for one whose heart was given to a different muse. I was usually examined in this author by the Senator's nephew, my fellow-student, whom I examined in turn; but once, at least, the Senator himself catechized me, though he presently began to talk about the four great English quarterly reviews which I was known in the village for reading, and which it seemed he read too. No doubt he found me more perfect in them than in Blackstone; at least I felt that I did myself more credit in them. I have elsewhere spoken more fully already of this episode of my life; but I speak of it again because I think that the commonly accepted Wade legend scarcely does justice to a man not only of great native power, but of wider cultivation than it recognizes, and I would like to do what I can to repair the injustice. He was famed in contemporary politics as Old Ben Wade before he had passed middle life, and he was supposed to stand up against the fierce pro-slavery leaders in Congress with an intrepidity even with their own. He had a strong, dark face, and a deep, raucous voice, with a defiant laugh, and these lent their support to the popular notion of him as a rude natural force unhelped by teaching, though he had taught himself in the days of his early struggle, as Lincoln and most public men of his time had done, and later had taught others as country schoolmaster. Farm-boy and cattle-drover and canal-digger, more had remained to him from schoolmaster and medical student, than from either of his other callings, and though he became part of our history without the help of great intellectual refinement, he was by no means without intellectual refinement, or without the ability to estimate the value of it in others. Naturally he might also underestimate it, and perhaps it was from an underestimate that he judged the oratory of such a man as Charles Sumner, to whom he told me he had said of a speech of his, "It's all very well, Sumner, but it has no bones in it."

Wade was supposed by his more ill-advised admirers to lend especial effect to his righteous convictions by a free flow of profanity, but I have to bear witness that I never heard any profanity from him, though profanity must have been the common parlance of the new country and the rude conditions he grew up in. He was personally a man of silent dignity, as we saw him in the village, going and coming at the post-office, for he seldom seemed to pass the gate of his house yard on any other errand, in the long summer vacations between the sessions of the many Congresses when he sojourned among us. I have the sense of him in a back room of the office which stood apart from his house, after the old-fashioned use of country lawyers' and doctors' offices; and I can be sure of his visiting the students in the front room only that once when he catechized me in Blackstone, but I cannot say whether I stood in awe of him as a great lawyer, or quite realized his importance as United States Senator from the State of Ohio for eighteen years. Historically it has been thought his misfortune to outlive the period when the political struggle with slavery passed into the Civil War, and to carry into that the spirit of the earlier time, with his fierce alienation from the patient policy of Lincoln, and his espousal of the exaggerations of the Reconstruction. But it would be easy to do injustice to this part of his valiant career, and not easy to do justice to that part of it where he stood with the very few in his defiance of the pro-slavery aggression.

Probably he would not have understood my forsaking the law, and I evaded the explanation he once sought of me when we met in the street, dreading the contempt which I might well have fancied in him. I wish now that, knowing him a little on his æsthetic side, I might have had the courage to tell him why I could not give my heart to that jealous mistress, being vowed almost from my first days to that other love which will have my fealty to the last. But in the helplessness of youth I could not even imagine doing this, and I had to remain in my dread of his contempt. Yet he may not have despised me, after all. It was known with what single-handed courage I was carrying on my struggle with the alien languages, and their number was naturally over-stated. The general interest in my struggle was reflected in the offer of a farmer from another part of the county to be one of three or four who would see me through Harvard. It was good-will which, if it had ever materialized, my pride would have been fierce to refuse; but now I think of it' without shame, and across the gulf which I would fain believe has some thither shore I should like to send that kind man the thanks which I fancy were never adequately expressed to him while he lived. It remains vaguely, from vague personal knowledge, that he was of Scotch birth and breeding; he had a good old Scotch name, and he lived on his prosperous farm in much more than the usual American state, with many books about him.

I went back not without shame, but also not without joy from the Senator's law-office to my father's printing-office, and I did not go to Harvard, or to any college or school thereafter. I still think that a pity, for I have never agreed with Lowell, who, when I deplored my want of schooling, generously instanced his own over-weight of learning as an evil I had escaped. It still seems to me lamentable that I should have had to grope my way and so imperfectly find it where a little light from another's lamp would have instantly shown it. I still remain in depths of incredible ignorance as to some very common things; for at school I never got beyond long division in arithmetic, and after my self-discovery of grammar I should be unable to say, *in due piedi*, just what a preposition was, though I am aware of frequently using that part of speech, and, I hope, not incorrectly.

I did what I could to repair the defect of instruction, or rather I tried to make myself do it, for I had the nature of a boy to contend with, and did not love my work so much as I loved the effect of it. While I live I must regret that want of instruction, and the discipline which

110

would have come with it, though Fortune, as if she would have flattered my vanity when she could bring her wheel round to it, bore me the offer of professorships in three of our greatest universities. In fact, when I thought of coming home from my consulship in Venice, ten years after my failure to achieve any sort of schooling, it had been my hope that I might get some sort of tutorship in a very modest college, and I wrote to Lowell about it, but he did not encourage me. Yet I was hardly fixed in the place which much better suited me as the assistant editor of the *Atlantic Monthly*, when one of the faculty came to me from Schenectady to offer me the sub-professorship of English in Union College, and no long time after I was sounded by the first educational authority in the country as to whether I would accept a like place in Washington University at St. Louis. It was twice as long after this that those three supreme invitations which I have boasted came to me. But I knew better than any one, unless it was Fortune herself, the ignorance I had hidden so long, and I forbore to risk a middling novelist on the chance of his turning out a poor professor, or none. In every case the offer was such as might well have allured me, but when, after a sleepless night of longing and fearing over that of Harvard which Lowell conveyed me with the promise, "You shall wear the gown that Ticknor wore, and Longfellow wore, and I wore," I had the strength to refuse it, he wrote me his approval of my decision. It was a decision that I have rejoiced in ever since, with the breathless gratitude, when I think of it, of one who has withheld himself from a step over the brink of a precipice.

The other allurements to a like doom were hardly less gratifying. What indeed could have been more gratifying, except the Harvard offer of the professorship of the languages of the south of Europe (with the privilege of

two years' preparation in the Latin countries, whose
tongues I had tampered with), than the offer of the English professorship in Yale? It was Lounsbury, now lately lost forever to these skies, Lounsbury the fine scholar,
the charming writer, the delightful wit, the critic unsur-
passed in his kind, who came smiling with the kind eyes,
dimmed almost to blindness on the field of Gettysburg
in the forgotten soldiership of his youth, to do me this
incredible honor. Later came the offer of the same chair
in Johns Hopkins, twice repeated by the president of
that university. When in my longing and my despair
I asked, What was the nature of such a professorship,
he answered, Whatever I chose to make it; and this still
seems to me, however mistaken in my instance, the very
measure of the wisest executive large-mindedness. President Gilman had written to me from New York, and had
come to see me in London, and again written to me in
Boston, and I could not do less than go down to Baltimore and look at the living body of the university and
see what part in it I might become. A day sufficed; where
so many men were busy with the work which they were
so singularly qualified to do, I could not think of bringing my half-heartedness to an attempt for which all the
common sense I had protested my unfitness, my entire
unlikeness to the kind of man he had so magnanimously
misimagined me. I turned from that shining opportunity of failure as I turned from the others, and if the
reader thinks I have dwelt too vaingloriously upon them
he shall have his revenge in the spectacle of my further
endeavors not to be the stuff which professors are made of.

XII

I could have been spared from the printing-office for
the study of the law, when I could not be spared from it

otherwise, because I might soon begin to make my living by practising before justices of the peace in the pettifogging which was then part of the study in the country offices. My labor, which was worth as much as a journeyman compositor's, could not have been otherwise spared; much less could my father have afforded the expense of my schooling; and I cannot recall that I thought it an unjust hardship when it was decided after due family counsel, that I could not be sent to an academy in a neighboring village. I had not the means of estimating my loss; but the event seemed to have remained a poignant regret with my brother, and in after years he lamented what he felt to have been an irreparable wrong done me: now he is dead, and it touches me to think he should have felt that, for I never blamed him, and I am glad he gave me the chance to tell him so. I may have shed some tears when first denied; I did shed a few very bitter ones when I once confessed the hope I had that the editor of the *Ohio Farmer* might give me some sort of literary employment at a sum I named, and he said, "He would never pay you three dollars a week in the world for that," and I had to own in anguish of soul that he was doubtless right. He worked every day of the week and far into every night to help my father earn the property we were all trying to pay for, and he rightfully came into the eventual ownership of the newspaper. By an irony of fate not wholly unkind he continued for half a century in the printing-business, once so utterly renounced. Then, after a few years of escape to a consular post in the tropics which he used to say was the one post which, if it had been whittled out of the whole universe, would have suited him best, he died, and lies buried in the village, the best-beloved man who ever lived there.

It was the day with us of self-denials which I cannot

trust myself to tell in detail lest I should overtell them. I was willing to make a greater figure in dress than nature has ever abetted me in, but I still do not think it was from an excess of vanity that I once showed my father the condition of my hat, and left him to the logic of the fact. He whimsically verified it, and said, "Oh, get it half-soled," as if it had been a shoe; and we had our laugh together, but I got the new hat, which, after all, did not make me the dashing presence I might have hoped, though the vision of it on the storekeeper's counter always remained so distinct with me that in Seville, a few years ago, it seemed as if its ghost were haunting me in the Cordovese hats on all the heads I met. Like them it had a wide flat brim, and it narrowed slightly upward to the low flat crown of those hats which I now knew better than to buy.

But if we seem to have spared on dress, our table was of as unstinted abundance as it might be in a place where there was no market, except as the farmers brought us chickens and butter and vegetables and the small fruits of the pastures and clearings, where every sort of wild berries grew. The region had abounded in deer, and after we came to the village in 1852 venison was only three cents a pound. Once a black bear was chased from forest to forest across our land, but he did not wait to fix the market price of his meat; half the sky was often hidden with wild pigeons, and there was a summer when the gray squirrels swarmed through the streets in one of their mystical migrations from west to east. Such chances of game scarcely enriched our larder; and the salt-pork barrel was our constant reliance. This was a hardship, after the varied abundance of the larger places where we had lived, but we shared it with our fellow-villagers, and in this as in other conditions of our life we did not realize as deprivation what was the lot of the whole community. If we denied ourselves it was

114

to meet the debts which would not be denied, and to possess ourselves of the roof over our heads and an ampler future in the ownership of our means of living. But I think we denied ourselves too much, and that we paid far beyond its moral worth for the house we were buying. To own the house she lived in had always been my mother's dream since her young married days when my father built the first little house where they dwelt together, and where I was born. In all the intervening quarter of a century they had lived in rented houses, and she could not help feeling that the rent they paid ought to have gone toward buying a house of their own. In this she was practically right, but now the house which we all worked so hard to buy belongs to strangers, and unless there is an effect of our self-denial in some other world, the purchase was as much waste as rent paid to a landlord. We were in fact always paying a certain rent in the interest on the notes which we slowly accumulated the money to meet, but my mother could not feel that the same, and I am glad she had her wish long before she died, and her last years were passed under a roof which she owned.

In time, but I do not know how long time, for such things did not interest me, though I was doing my share in helping pay off our debt, the promissory notes which my father had given for the purchase of our newspaper were taken up, and the newspaper was also our property. Nobody could molest us or make us afraid in its possession; and in my hope of other things it did not concern me that the title vested in his partnership with my brother, who had most justly earned his half, and who by an enterprise of his own finally established the family fortunes in un-dreamed-of prosperity. It was characteristic of my father that as long as their partnership existed there were no accounts between them; after my brother had a family of his own each drew from the common income at his wish

115

or need, and when I came of sufficient worldly wisdom to realize the risks to their peace from this anomalous arrangement, I protested against it in vain. They agreed with me that it was precarious and in a way ridiculous, and that it certainly ought to cease, but as long as they continued together they remained partners on these terms. After my father withdrew, my brother took his own son into partnership, and when he came in his turn to retire, he contritely owned to me that they had not departed from the same old unbusiness-like community of ways and means, though he had promised me very earnestly many times to end it. While I am upon these matters it is a pleasure for me to record that when I came home from Venice with the manuscript of *Venetian Life* promised publication by a London house if I could find an American house to take half the proposed edition, and I confessed that I had very little hope of getting this taken in New York or Boston, my brother promptly offered to take it himself. He was then in that undreamed-of prosperity which I have mentioned, and though he had no expectation of becoming a book-publisher, he was very willing to incur the risks involved. As all my world knows, the book found an equally courageous friend in New York, and came out with the American imprint of Hurd & Houghton instead of Joseph A. Howells & Co.

It is not surprising to me that I cannot date the time of our acquiring the newspaper, free and clear, as the real-estate phrase is, but I am certainly surprised and more pained that I cannot remember just when the house, endeared to us as home, became our very own. Its possession, as I have said, had been the poetry of my mother's hard-working, loving life, and no doubt she had watched with hope and fear the maturing of each of the notes for it, with the interest they bore, until the last was paid off. In my father's buoyant expectation of the best in everything, I do not think he had any misgiving of the event; my brother must have shared my mother's anxiety, but we younger children did not, and the great hour arrived without record in my consciousness. Years later, when I came back from long sojourn abroad, I found that the little ground-wren's nest, as it looks to me in the retrospect, had widened by half a dozen rooms without rising above its original story and a half. All round it the garden space was red and purple with the grapes which my father had induced, by his steady insistence, the neighboring farmers to plant. My mother and he were growing sweetly old in the keeping of the place, and certain wild furred and feathered things had come to share their home with them. Not only the door-yard trees which we boys had brought from the woods had each its colony of birds, but in the eaves a family of flying-squirrels had nested. I do not know whether I can impart the sense of peace and security which seemed to have spread from the gentle household to them, but I am sure that my mother could not have realized a fonder vision of the home she had longed for through so many years.

XIII

I do not think my father so much cared for the ownership of the newspaper. He took our enterprise more easily than my elder brother, but that was temperamental in both, and one was no more devoted than the other. My companionship was far more with my father, but before my intimacy with J. W. interrupted this my studies had already ascertained the limits of his learning in the regions where I was groping my way, and where the light of my friend's greater knowledge now made him my guide. If J. W. was more definite in his ambition of one day getting some sort of college professorship than I in my plans of literary achievement, he could not have been more intense in his devotion to what we were trying to do. I was studying those languages because I wished to possess myself of their literatures; still groping my way in the dark, where a little light shed from larger learning would have helped me so much. The grammars and the text-books could tell me what I wanted to know, but they did not teach it; and I realize now as I could not then that self-taught is half-taught. Yet I think my endeavor merited reward; if I worked blindly, I worked hard; and in my attempts at fiction or at verse where I could create the light by mere trituration, as it were, I did not satisfy myself with less than final perfection so far as I could imagine it. I loved form, I loved style, I loved diction, and I strove for them all, rejecting my faultier ideals when I discovered them, and cleaving to the truer. In some things, the minor things, I was of wavering preference; I wrote a different hand every other week, and if I have now an established handwriting it is more from disgust of change than from preference. In the spirit of my endeavor there was no variableness; always I strove for grace, for distinctness, for light; and my soul detests obscurity still. That is perhaps why I am beating out my meaning here at the risk of beating it into thin air.

In the final judgment of my father's help and unhelp in my endeavors, I should say that they were the measure of his possibility. For a man of his conditioning he had a wonderful outlook in many directions on life, but he was without perspective; he could not see how my unaided efforts were driving to the vanishing-point. He had been my instructor in many things beyond my young ken; he had an instinct for beauty and truth; he loved the poetry which was the best in his youth, though he did not deny me the belief that the poetry of mine was better still; his gentle intelligence could follow me where

118

his liking failed, and he modestly accepted my opinions. His interest had once been absorbed mostly, but not wholly, by the faith which he had imbibed from his reading of Swedenborg, but when I began to know him as a boy may know his elder, he was more and more concerned in the national struggle with the pro-slavery aggression. Politics had always been his main worldly interest, and not only as to measures; he passionately favored certain men, because he liked the nature of them, as well as because he believed them right. It seems to me now that he took a personal interest in conventions and nominations, but I am not sure, for I myself took no interest whatever in them; their realities did not concern me so much as the least unrealities of fiction; and I can only make sure of my father's interest in the elections after the nominations. I suppose that he was not very skilled in practical politics, as log-rolling and wire-pulling have come to be called, though in a village which was the home of a United States Senator, a Congressional Representative, a State Senator, and a Legislative Representative, with the full corps of county office-holders, and a Common Pleas Judge, the science might well have forced itself upon his study. Many years after our coming to the Western Reserve he was sent to the State Senate by a war-majority larger than any majority which had yet returned a candidate, or yet has; but long before that he began to find his way beyond the local favor or disfavor, and was chosen one of the House clerks in the State Legislature. That must have been when I was eighteen years old, but he seems to have left our newspaper to my sole charge without misgiving, and fortunately no trouble came of his trust in me. I was then taking my civic and social opinions from the more Tory of the English quarterlies, but nobody knew what I meant by them; I did not know myself, and I did no harm with them.

In the mean time our Congressman was writing for us every week from Washington a letter full of politics far more intelligible to our readers than mine were to me. He was that Joshua R. Giddings, early one of the paladins of anti-slavery in a series of pro-slavery Congresses, where he represented and distinguished his district for twenty years after his resignation under a vote of censure and his overwhelming re-election. But in a fatal moment of that fatigue which comes to elderly people, he finally let fall an expression of indifference to office. The minor and meaner men of his party who were his enemies promptly seized the chance of defeating him for the nomination which was equivalent to an election in our district, and an inferior good man was named in his place. His friends would have had him contest the decision of the convention, but he would not, and he passed into private life, where he remained till the favor of Lincoln sought him out, and he died Consul-General to Canada after he had lived to write several books and to tell the story of the Civil War up to its penultimate year. Neither he nor Wade was of that Connecticut lineage which almost exclusively peopled the Western Reserve, and especially in Ashtabula County desired power and place to itself. Wade was from western Massachusetts, and Giddings was from western Pennsylvania, but in the new country where they met, they joined their forces as partners in the law, and remained together till politics separated them in the same cause. They still remained fellow-citizens of the little town where they spent the summer leisure of the Congressional adjournments, but without, somehow I imagine, seeing much of each other. Giddings was far more freely about the place, where his youth had been passed in the backwoods, and where he made himself familiarly at home. The very simplicity of the place seemed to comport with his statesman-like presence, his noble head, and his great Johnsonian face, when he came out of his large old-fashioned dwelling, sole rival of the Wade mansion; and he had no need to stoop in being fellow-citizen with the least of his constituents. For myself, I cannot recall any passage of words with him after a forgotten introduction, and I wish it had been otherwise. I wish now I could have known him even as a boy in his middle teens may know a man of his make; though he might not have said anything to me worth remembering, or inspired me to any expression worthier the event than that of a Louisianian whom long later I saw introduced to him in Columbus, at his own request. The Southerner stared at the giant bulk of the man who must have long embodied to his imagination a demoniacal enmity to his section, and could think of nothing better to say than, "Very pretty day, Mr. Giddings," and when Giddings had assented with, "Yes, sir, a fine day," the interview ended.

"Giddings, far rougher names than thine have grown
    Smoother than honey on the lips of men,"

Lowell wrote in one of those magnanimous sonnets of his, when he bent from his orient height to the brave Westerner, and though it has not yet come quite to that honeyed utterance, the name cannot be forgotten when the story of our Civil War, with its far or near beginnings, is told.

XIV

That winter of my editorship wore away to the adjournment of the legislature and my father's return home, after J. W.'s withdrawal into the vague of Wisconsin. But now another beloved friend had come to us. He had learned his trade with us in southern Ohio, where he lived with our family like one of ourselves, as brotherly as if he had been of our blood. In those days he and I read the same books and dreamed the same dreams, but he was nearer my eldest brother in age, and was as much his companion as mine. After he left us to live the wander-years of the journeyman printer, we heard from him at different points where he rested, and when the Civil War began in Kansas, five years before it began in South Carolina, we knew of him fighting and writing on the Free State side. In this time, my brother made it his romance to promote a correspondence between H. G. and a young girl of the village, which ended in their engagement. It was taking too great a risk in every way, but they were fitly mated in their tastes, and their marriage was of such lasting attachment that when she survived him and lay suffering in her last sickness, she prayed every night that she might die before she woke and be with him in the everlasting morning. Romance for romance, I think their romance of the greatest pathos of any I have known, and it had phases of the highest tragedy. H. G. was among the first to volunteer for the great war, and quickly rose from the ranks to be captain, but somehow he incurred the enmity of a superior officer who was able to have him cashiered in dishonor from the army. The great war which we look back upon as hallowed by a singleness of patriotic purpose was marked by many private wrongs which were promptly revenged, or kept for ultimate vengeance, sometimes forgone at last through the wearing out of the hate which cherished them. I am glad to think this was so with H. G.; his memory is very dear to me, and our friendship was of a warmth of affection such as I did not know for J. W., though he had so much greater charm for me, and in the communion of our minds I was so much more intimate with him.

YEARS OF MY YOUTH

Earlier in his absence, I had grown more and more into intellectual companionship with the eldest of my sisters, who was only little more than a year younger than myself. We had gone to the village parties and dances and sleigh-rides together, but she was devoted to my mother and the helper in her work, and gave herself far less than I to the pleasures which had palled upon me; she may never have cared for them much; certainly not so much as for the household life. It is one of those unavailing regrets which gather upon us if we question memory as I am doing now, and try to deal honestly with the unsparing truth of its replies, that I ignored so long her willingness to be my companion in the things of the mind. With my mother it was a simple affair; I was bound to her in an affection which was as devoted throughout my youth as it had been in my childhood; she was herself the home which I suffered such longing for if I ever left it; and I am now, in my old age, humbly grateful for the things I was prompted to do in my love of her. I could not, without an effect of exaggeration unworthy of her dear memory, express my sense of her motherly perfection within the limits of her nature, which I would not now have had different through worldly experience or privilege. She had, like my father, the instinct of poetry; and over what was left of her day's work for the long evenings which we spent reading or talking or laughing together, while my father selected copy for his paper without losing the fun we all made, she was gay with the gayest of us. Often I had savagely absented myself from the rest, but when I came out of my little study, dazed with my work, after the younger children had gone to bed, I have the vision of her rolling her sewing together in her lap, and questioning me with her fond eyes what I was thinking of or had been trying to do.

I believe she did not ask; that was forbidden by my

123

pride and shame. I did not read to any of them what I had been writing; they would not have been hard enough upon it to satisfy me, though if they had criticized it I should have been furious. In fact, I was not an amiable or at least a reasonable youth; it was laid upon me to try solitarily for the things I had no help in doing, and I seldom admitted any one to the results until that sister of mine somehow passed my ungracious reserves. I do not know just how this happened; but perhaps it was through our confiding to each other, brokenly, almost unspokenly, our discontent with the village limit of our lives. Within our home we had the great world, at least as we knew it in books, with us, but outside of it, our social experience dwindled to the measure of the place. I have tried to say how uncommon the place was intellectually, but we disabled it on that side because it did not realize the impossible dreams of that great world of wealth, of fashion, of haughtily and dazzlingly, blindingly brilliant society, which we did not inconveniently consider we were altogether unfit for. The reader may or may not find a pathos in our looking at the illustration on the front of a piece of tawdry sheet-music, and wondering whether it would ever be our high fortune to mingle with a company of such superbly caparisoned people as we saw pictured there, playing and singing and listening.

Vanity so criminal as ours, might have been for a just punishment lastingly immured in that village which the primeval woods encircled like a prison wall; and yet almost at that moment, when we had so tardily discovered ourselves akin in our tastes, our hopes and despairs, we were nearer the end of our imprisonment than we could have imagined. Whether we were punished in our enlargement which we were both so near, I cannot say; my own life since that time has been such as some know and any may know who care, and of hers I may scarcely speak. After a few happy weeks, a few happy months of our common escape, she went back to those bounds where her duty lay; and when after many years she escaped from them again it was to circumstances where she was so willingly useful as to feel herself very happy. Her last dream, one of being usefuler yet to those dearest to her, ended in a nightmare of disappointment; but that too had wholly passed before she woke to the recompense which we try to believe that death shall bring to all who suffer here to no final good.

Now it was life full beyond our fondest expectations, if not our fancies of its possibilities, which lured us forward. We were making the most of our mutual interest in the books we were reading, and she was giving, as sisters give so far beyond the giving of brothers, her sympathy to me in what I was trying to write. It was some time since I had turned, upon the counsel of J. W., from Greek to German, I forget from just what reasoning, though I think it was because he said I could study Greek any time, and now we could study German together. I had gone so far with it that I was already reading Heine and trying to write like him, instead of reading my Spanish poets and trying to imitate them in their own meters. But there is scarcely any definite memory of my sister's literary companionship left me. I remember her coming to me once with the praise, which I shamefacedly refused, of the neighbor who had pointed to a row of Washington Irving's works in her house, and said that some day my books would fill a shelf like that. For the rest, I am dimly aware of our walking summer evenings down a certain westward way from our house, and of her helping me dream a literary future. If she had then a like ambition she kept it from me, and it was not till twenty years later that she sent me a play she had written, with village motives and village realities, treated with a frankness which I still had not the intelligence to value. The play never came to the stage, and in that farther time, it was the fruition of hopes which had not defined themselves, that when my father's scheme was realized, not only I, but she too, was to return to Columbus with him. It would be easy to pretend, and I can easily believe that we had always, at the bottom of our hearts, thought of Columbus with distinct longing; but I am not sure that there was more in our remembrance of it than a sense of its greatness as the state capital to give direction to our ambition for some experience of the world beyond our village. There was no part for her in our journalistic plan; probably the affair for her was an outing which she had won by her unselfish devotion to the duties of her narrow lot; but what I am sure of, and what I am glad of now, amidst my compunctions for not valuing her loving loyalty at its true worth, is that she did have this outing.

III

THROUGHOUT his later boyhood and into his earlier manhood the youth is always striving away from his home and the things of it. With whatever pain he suffers through the longing for them, he must deny them; he must cleave to the world and the things of it; that is his fate, that is the condition of all achievement and advancement for him. He will be many times ridiculous and sometimes contemptible, he will be mean and selfish upon occasion; but he can scarcely otherwise be a man; the great matter for him is to keep some place in his soul where he shall be ashamed. Let him not be afraid of being too unsparing in his memories; the instinct of self-preservation will safeguard him from showing himself quite as he was. No man, unless he puts on the mask of fiction, can show his real face or the will behind it. For this reason the only real biographies are the novels, and every novel, if it is honest, will be the autobiography of the author and biography of the reader.

I

It was doubtless a time of intense emotion for our whole family when my sister and I set out for the state capital with my father on his return to his clerical duties at the meeting of the legislature in 1856. If I cannot make sure that Columbus had become with those of us old enough to idealize it, a sort of metropolis of the mind to which we should repair if we were good enough, or, failing that, if fortune were ever kind enough, I am certain that my father's sojourn there, with his several visits to us during the winter before, had kept the wonder of it warm in my heart. The books that he brought me at each return from the State Library renewed in me the sense of a capital which he had tried to implant in me when we lived there, and my sister could not have dreamt of anything grander or gayer. Perhaps we both still saw ourselves there in scenes like that in the title-page of that piece of sheet-music; but anything so definite as this I cannot be sure of.

What I can be sure of is the substantial nature and occasion of our going, so far as I was concerned. "We were to furnish," my father and I, as I have told in *My Literary Passions*, "a daily letter giving an account of the legislative proceedings, which I was mainly to write from material he helped me get together. The letters at once found favor with the editors, who agreed to take them, and my father then withdrew from the work, after telling them who was doing it." My sister of course had no part in the enterprise, and for her our adventure was pure pleasure, the pleasure we both took in our escape from the village, and the pleasure I did not understand then that she had in witnessing my literary hopes and labors.

In like manner I am belatedly sensible of the interest which our dear H. G. took in our going, and the specific instructions which he gave me for my entry into the great world; as if he would realize in my prosperous future the triumphs which fortune had denied him in his past. He adjured me not to be abashed in any company, but face the proudest down and make audacity do the part of the courage I was lacking in. Especially he would have me not distrust myself in such a social essential as dancing, which was a grace I was confessedly imperfect in, but to exhaust the opportunities of improving it which the Saturday evening hops at our hotel would give me. He advised me not to dress poorly, but go to the full length of Polonius's precept—

"Costly thy habit as thy purse can buy"—

though what advantages his own experiences in these matters had won him could not have been very signal. He knew my ambition in that way, and how it had been defeated by the friendly zeal of our home-tailor; and we both held that with the clothing-stores of High Street open to my money all I had to do was to fix my mind upon a given suit which would fit me as perfectly as the Jew said, and then wear it away triumphantly appareled for the highest circles. We did not know that the art of dressing well, or fashionably, comes from deep and earnest study, and that the instinct of it might well have been blunted in me by my Quaker descent, with that desire to shine rather in the Other World than in this which had become a passion with my grandfather.

No fact of my leaving home upon the occasion which I must have felt so tremendous remains with me. I cannot even say whether it was through the snow or the mud that we drove ten miles from the county-seat to the railroad station at Ashtabula; whatever the going, it was over the warped and broken boards of the ancient plank-road which made any transit possible in that region of snow and mud, and remained till literally worn away even in the conception of the toll-taker. Without intervening event, so far as my memory testifies, or circumstance, any more than if we had flown through the air, we were there in Columbus together, living in an old-fashioned hotel on the northward stretch of High Street,

129

which was then the principal business street, and for anything I know is so yet. The hotel was important to the eye of our village strangeness, but it was perhaps temperamentally of the sort of comfortable taverns which the hotels had come to displace. My father had gone to live there because he knew it from our brief sojourn when we came to the city from the country five or six years before, and because it was better suited to his means; but one of the vividest impressions of his youth had been the building of the National Road, a work so monumental for the new country it traversed, and he poetically valued the Goodale House for facing upon this road, which in its course from Baltimore to St. Louis became High Street in Columbus.

Not even in this association could it be equaled with the Neil House, then the finest hotel in the West, without a peer even in Cincinnati. Dickens, in his apparently unreasoned wanderings, paused in it over a day, and admired its finish in black-walnut, the wood that came afterward to be so precious for the ugliest furniture ever made. All visitors of distinction sojourned there, and it was the resort of the great politicians who held their conclaves in its gloomy corridors and in its office and bar on the eve of nominating conventions or the approach of general elections. I have a vision, which may be too fond, of their sitting under its porches in tilted arm-chairs as the weather softened, canvassing the civic affairs which might not have been brought to a happy issue without them. But however misled I may be in this I cannot err in my vision of the stately conflagration which went up with the hotel one windless night, a mighty front of flame hooded with somber smoke. I watched it with a vast crowd from the steps of the State House which it was worthier to face than any other edifice of the little city; but this was long after that

130

winter of ours in the Goodale House, which I remember for the boundless abundance of its table and for those society events which on Saturday nights crowned the week.

I dare say they were not so fashionable as H. G. imagined them, or I, with a heart too weak and feet too untutored ever to join in them, but the world was present in other sophistications in our pleasant hotel which I could not so easily shun. Chief of these was the tipping, which there first insisted on my acquaintance by many polite insinuations, and when I would have withdrawn became explicit. The kind colored waiter who used to cumber me with service at table as his anxieties mounted once took courage to whisper in my ear that he thought he would like to go to the theater that evening, and it grieves me yet to think that I resented this freedom, and denied him the quarter he suggested. Since then life has been full of the experiences of tipping, always so odious, though apparently more rapacious than it really is, but I have never again been able to deny a tip, or to give so little as I would often like to give. I know that some better citizens, or wiser, than myself, punish the neglect or ingratitude of service by diminishing or withholding the tip, but I have never been able to perform this public-spirited duty, perhaps because, though I loathe tipping, I do not believe any fellow-creature

"As meek and mere a serving-man,"

as may be, would take a tip if he were paid a just wage, or any wage, without it.

But all these incidents and interests were far in the future of that brave and happy time when I was intending and attempting the conquest of the whole field of polite learning from so many sides, in the studies which as at home now went on far into the night. These even included an Icelandic grammar, for the reason that, as I had read, the meter of *Hiawatha* was derived from that literature, but I do not know that I got so far as to identify it. My reading, now entirely from the State Library, included all the novels of Bulwer, which I was not ashamed to enjoy after my more distinguished pleasure in Thackeray; the critical authorities would not then have abashed me in it, as they would now. The other day I saw on my shelves the volume of *Percy's Reliques* which my sister and I read together that winter; and I was so constantly and devotedly reading Tennyson and Shakespeare that I cannot understand how I had time for an equal constancy and devotion to Heine. I saw how much he had profited by the love of those English ballads which I was proud to share with him; and there were other German poets of his generation whose indebtedness to them I perceived and enjoyed. I was now, in fact, reading German to the entire neglect of Spanish; as for Latin and Greek, I had no more time or relish for them than those cultivated gentlemen who believe they read some Latin or Greek author every day before breakfast.

II

The life and the letters continued on terms which I should not have known how to wish different. I had a desk appointed me on the floor of the Senate as good as any Senator's, for my convenience as a reporter; and my father gave me notes of the proceedings in the House, so that I could make a fair report of each day's facts which we so early abandoned the pretense of his making. Every privilege and courtesy was shown the press, which sometimes I am afraid its correspondents accepted ungraciously. Either the first winter or the next one of them was expelled from the floor of the House for his over-bold criticisms of some member, and I espoused his cause with quite outrageous zeal. I had, indeed, such a swollen ideal of the rights and duties of the press that I spared no severity in my censure of Senators I found misguided. I was, perhaps, not wholly fitted by my nineteen years to judge them, though this possibility did not occur to me at the time with its present force; but if I was not impressed with the dignity of the Senate, the dignity of the Senate Chamber was a lasting effect with me, as, in fact, that of the whole Capitol was. I seemed to share personally in it as I mounted the stately marble stairway from the noble rotunda or passed through the ample corridors from the Senate to the House where it needed not even a nod to the sergeant-at-arms to gain me access to the floor; a nonchalant glance was enough. But the grandeur of the interior, which I enjoyed with the whole legislative body, was not more wonderful than its climate, which I found tempered against the winter to a summer warmth by the air rushing from the furnaces in the basement through gratings in the walls and floors. These were for me the earliest word of the comfort that now pervades our whole well-warmed American world, but I had scarcely imagined them even from my father's report. How could I imagine them or fail to attribute to myself something like merit from them? I enjoyed, in fact, something like moral or civic ownership of the whole place, which I penetrated in every part on my journalistic business: the court-rooms, the agricultural department, the executive offices, and how do I know but the very room of the Governor himself? The library was of course my personal resort; as I have told, I was always getting books from it, and these books had a quality in coming from the State Library which intensified my sense of being of, as well as in, the capital of Ohio.

Whether the city itself shared my sense of its importance

in the same measure I am not sure. There were reasons, however, why it might have done so. It was then what would be now a small city, say not above twenty thousand, and though it had already begun to busy itself with manufacturing and had two or three railroads centering in it, the industries and facilities which have now swollen its population to almost a quarter of a million were then in their beginning. Its political consciousness may have been the greater, therefore; it may indeed have been subjectively the sovereign city which I so objectively felt it. In that time, in fact, a state capital was both comparatively and positively of greater reality than it has been since. With the Civil War carried to its close in the reconstituted Union, the theory of State Rights forever vanished, and with this the dignity which once clothed the separate existence of the states. Their shadowy sovereignty had begun to wane in the anti-slavery North because it was the superstition of the pro-slavery South, yet I can remember a moment when there was much talk, though it never came to more than talk, of turning this superstition to a faith and applying it to the defeat of the Fugitive Slave Law. If it was once surmised that the decisions of the Ohio courts might nullify a law of the United States I do not believe that this surmise ever increased the political consciousness of our state capital. It remained a steadily prospering town like other towns, till now perhaps it may not feel itself a capital at all. Perhaps it could be restored to something like the quality I valued in it by becoming the residence of envoys from the other state capitals, and sending a minister to each of these. I have the conviction that public-spirited citizens could be found to take such offices at very moderate salaries, and that their wives would be willing to aid in restoring the shadow of state sovereignty by leaving cards upon one another.

The winter of 1856–57 passed without my knowing more of the capital than its official world. Even the next year, when I began to make some acquaintance with the social world, it was with an alien or adoptive phase of it, as I realize with tardy surprise. There were then so many Germans in Ohio that an edition of the laws had to be printed in their language, and there was a common feeling that we ought to know their language, if not their literature, which was really what I cared more to know. I carried my knowledge of it so far as to render a poem of my own into German verse which won the praise of my teacher; and I wish I could remember who he was, gentle, tobacco-smoked shade that he has long since become, or who the German editor of what *republikanische Zeitung* was that sometimes shared my instruction with him. There were also two blithe German youths who availed with me in the loan of Goethe's *Wahlverwandschaft-en*, and gave me some fencing lessons in their noonings. I forget what employ they were of, but their uncle was a watchmaker and jeweler, and my father got him to gold-plate his silver watch, or dye it, as he preferred to say. When the Civil War came he went into it and was killed; and many years afterward, in my love and honor of him, I turned his ghost into a loved and honored character in *A Hazard of New Fortunes*. He was a political refugee, of those German revolutionists who came to us after the revolts of 1848, and he still dwells venerable in my memory, with his noble, patriarchally bearded head.

But it all appears very fantastic in the retrospect, that Teutonic period of my self-culture, and I am not sure that one fact of it is more fantastic than another. Such was my zeal for everything German that I once lunched at one of the German beer-saloons which rather abounded in Columbus, on Swiss cheese with French mustard spread over it and a tall glass of lager beer, then much valued as a possible transition from the use of the strong waters more habitual with Americans than now; but it made me very sick, and I was obliged to forego it as an expression of my love for German poetry. To a little earlier period must have belonged the incident of my going to see *"Die Räuber"* of Schiller, which I endured with iron resolution from the beginning to the end. It was given, I believe, by amateurs, and I tried my best to imagine that I understood it as it went on, but probably I did not, though I would have been loath to own the fact to any of the few German families who then formed my whole acquaintance with society. I never afterward met them at American houses; the cleavage between the two races in everything but politics was absolute; though the Germans were largely anti-slavery, and this formed common ground for them and natives of like thinking who did not know them socially.

In those first winters my knowledge of American society was confined to the generalized hospitality of the large evening receptions which some of the leading citizens used to give the two Houses of the legislature, including the correspondents and reporters attached to them. I cannot say just how or when I began to divine that these occasions were not of the first fashion, though the hosts and hostesses might have been so. There were great suppers, mainly of oysters, to which our distance from the sea lent distinction, and ice-cream, and sometimes, if I may trust a faint reverberation from the past as of blown corks, champagne. There was also dancing, and when some large, old-fashioned house was not large enough, a wooden pavilion was improvised over the garden to give the waltzes and quadrilles verge enough. I recall my share in the suppers, if not in the dancing, but my deficiency was far more than made up by the excess of a friend, who must then have been hard upon sixty years of age, yet was of a charming gaiety and an unimpaired youthfulness. He stood up in every quadrille, and he danced to the end of the evening, with a demure smile on his comely, smooth-shaven, rosy face, and a light, mocking self-consciousness in his kind eyes, as if he would agree as to any incongruity the spectator might find in his performance. He was one of the clerks of the House, an old politician, and the editor of a leading Cleveland newspaper, which he chose to leave for the pleasures of the capital. From his experience of the system which he was part of he whimsically professed to believe that as great legislative wisdom could be assembled by knocking down every other man in a crowd and dragging him into the House or Senate as by the actual method of nomination and election. At times he would support the theory of a benevolent despotism, and advocate the establishment of what he called a one-man power as the ideal form of government. I owed him much in the discharge of duties which my finding the most important in the world must have amused him, and when he went back to his newspaper he left me to write the legislative letters for it.

This gentle reactionary was the antithesis of another very interesting man, known to his fellow-legislators as Citizen Corry, in recognition of his preference for the type of French Red Republicanism acquired in Paris during his stay through the academic republic of 1848–50. Such a residence would alone have given him a distinction which we can hardly realize in our time, but he was, besides, a man of great natural distinction, and of more cultivation than any of his fellow-legislators. He was one of the Representatives from Cincinnati, and when another Cincinnati Representative of his own party struck a member from the Western Reserve, Citizen Corry joined the Republicans in voting his expulsion. But he had already made a greater sensation, and created an expectation of the unexpected in all he did by proposing an amendment to the Constitution abolishing the system of dual chambers in the legislature, and retaining only the House of Representatives. I think that in Greece alone is this the actual parliamentary form, but I believe that it was in that short-lived French republic of 1848 that Corry saw its workings and conceived the notion of its superiority. Under the present system he held that the House was merely a committee at the bar of the Senate, and the Senate a committee at the bar of the House, with a great waste of time and public advantage through the working of a very clumsy machinery. His proposition was not taken seriously by the Ohio House of Representatives, but to my young enthusiasm it seemed convincing by its mere statement, and the arguments on the other side, to the effect that the delays which he censured gave time for useful reflection, appeared to me very fallacious. Citizen Corry was not re-elected to the next legislature, and his somewhat meteoric history did not include any other official apparition. But while he was passing through the orbit of my world I was fully aware of his vivid difference from the controlled and orderly planets, and he dazzled in me an imagination always too fondly seeking the bizarre and strange. I do not think I ever spoke with him, but I tingled to do so; I created him citizen of that fine and great world where I had so much of my own being in reveries that rapt me from the realities of the life about me.

IV

The first winter of my legislative correspondence began with a letter to my Cincinnati newspaper in which I described the public opening of the new State House. I remember the event vividly because I thought it signally important, and partly because, to relieve myself from the stress of the crowd passing through the doorways, I lifted my arms and was near having my breath crushed out. There were a ball and a banquet, but somewhere, somehow, amidst the dancing and the feeding and smoking, I found a corner where I could write out my account of the affair and so escaped with my letter and my life.

Much as I might have wished to share socially, with such small splendor as might be, in this high occasion, the reporter's instinct was first with me. I was there as the representative of a great Cincinnati newspaper, and I cared more to please its management than to take any such part as I might in the festivity. My part was to look on and tell what I saw, and I must have done this in the manner of my most approved good masters, no doubt with satirically poetic touches from Heine and bits of worldly glitter from Thackeray. I should like to see that letter now, and I should like to know how I contrived to get it, more or less surreptitiously, into the hands of the express agent for delivery to my newspaper. In those days there was a good deal of talk, foolish talk, I am since aware, of having the post-office superseded in its functions by the express companies. Now the talk and the fact are all the other way; but then the mail was slow and uncertain, and if my letter was of the nature of manuscript the express might safely carry it and deliver it in time for the next day's paper. That was rightful and lawful enough, but there was a show of secrecy in the transaction which was not unpleasing to the enterprise of a young reporter.

My letters, as they went on from day to day, contented the managers of the *Gazette* so well that when the session of the legislature ended they gave me an invitation which

might well have abused my modesty with a sense of merit.
This invitation was to come and be their city editor, which
then meant the local reporting, at a salary twice as great
as that which I had been getting as their legislative correspondent. I do not know whose inspiration the offer
was, but I should like to believe it was that of the envoy
from the paper who made it in person, after perhaps
more fully satisfying himself of my fitness. He is long
since dead, but if he were still alive I hope he would
not mind my describing him as of less stature than
myself even, wearing the large, round glasses which
give certain near-sighted persons a staring look, and of
speech low almost to whispering, so that I could not
quite be sure that the incredible thing he was proposing
was really expressed to me. I like to recall the personal
fact of him because he was always my friend, and he
would have found me another place on the paper if he
could when I would not take the one he had offered. He
did make room for me in his own department for as long
as he could, or as I would stay, when I went down to
Cincinnati to look the ground over, and he kept me his
guest as far as sharing his room with me in the building
where we worked together, and where I used to grope
my way toward midnight up a stairway entirely black to
his door. There I lighted the candle-end which I found
within and did what I could to sleep till he came, hours
later, when the paper went to press. I have the belief
that the place was never swept or dusted, and that this
did not matter to the quiet, scholarly man whose life
was so wholly in his work that he did not care how he
lived.

He was buoyed up, above all other things, by the
interest of journalism, which for those once abandoned to
it is indeed a kind of enchantment. As I knew it then
and afterward, it has always had far more of my honor

and respect than those ignorant of it know how to render. One incident of it at this time so especially moved me that I will give it place in this wayward tale, though it is probably not more to the credit of the press than unnumbered others which others could cite. A miserable man came late one night to ask that a certain report which involved his good name, and with it the good name of a miserable woman, and the peace of their families, might be withheld. He came with legal counsel, and together they threshed the matter out with our editorial force upon the point whether we ought or ought not to spare him, our contention being that as a prominent citizen he was even less to be spared than a more unimportant person. Our professional conscience was apparently in that scruple; how it was overcome I do not remember, but at last we promised mercy and the report was suppressed.

It was one of the ironies of life that after the only suspected avenue to publicity had been successfully guarded, the whole fact should have cruelly come out in another paper the next morning. But I cannot feel even yet that the beauty of our merciful decision was marred by this mockery of fate, or that the cause of virtue was served by it, and I think that if I had been wiser than I was then I would have remained in the employ offered me, and learned in the school of reality the many lessons of human nature which it could have taught me. I did not remain, and perhaps I could not; it might have been the necessity of my morbid nerves to save themselves from abhorrent contacts; in any case, I renounced the opportunity offered me by that university of the streets and police-stations, with its faculty of patrolmen and ward politicians and saloon-keepers. The newspaper office was not the Capitol of Ohio; I was not by the fondest imputation a part of the state government, and I felt the dif-

YEARS OF MY YOUTH

ference keenly. I was always very homesick; I knew nobody in the city, and I had no companionship except that of my constant friend, whom I saw only in our hours of work. I had not even the poor social refuge of a boarding-house; I ate alone at a restaurant, where I used sadly to amuse myself with the waiters' versions of the orders which they called down a tube into the kitchen below. The one which cheered me most was that of a customer who always ordered a double portion of corn-cakes and was translated as requiring "Indians, six on a plate."

Nearly all the frequenters of this restaurant were men from their stores and offices, snatching a hasty midday meal, but a few were women, clerks and shop-girls of the sort who now so abound in our towns and cities, but then so little known. I was so altogether ignorant of life that I thought shame of them to be boldly showing themselves in such a public place as a restaurant. I wonder what they would have thought, poor, blameless dears, of the misgivings in the soul of the conscious youth as he sat stealing glances of injurious conjecture at them while he overate himself with the food which was the only thing that could appease for a moment the hunger of his homesick heart. If I could not mercifully imagine them, how could I intelligently endure the ravings of the drunken woman which I heard one night in the police-station where my abhorred duties took me for the detestable news of the place? I suppose it was this adventure, sole of its sort, which clinched my resolve to have no more to do with the money-chance offered to me in journalism. My longing was for the cleanly respectabilities, and I still cannot think that a bad thing, or if experience cannot have more than the goodly outside in life, that this is not well worth having. There was a relief, almost an atonement, or at least a consolation in being sent next

142

day to report a sermon, in fulfilment of my friend's ideal of journalistic enterprise, and though that sermon has long since gone from me and was perhaps at the time not distinctly with me, still I have a sense of cleansing from the squalor of the station-house in listening to it. If all my work could have been the reporting of sermons, with intervals of sketching the graduating ceremonies of young ladies' seminaries, such as that where once a girl in garnet silk read an essay of perhaps no surpassing interest, but remained an enchanting vision, and the material of some future study in fiction; if it could have been these things, with nothing of police-stations in it, I might have tried longer to become a city editor. But as it was I decided my destiny in life differently.

V

I must not conceal the disappointment which my father delicately concealed when I returned and took up my old work in the printing-office. He might well have counted on my help in easing him of his load of debt, from the salary I had forgone, but there was no hint of this in the welcome given me in the home where I was again so doubly at home with my books and manuscripts. Now and then my friend of the *Gazette* management managed to have some sketch of mine accepted for it, and my life went on in my sister's literary companionship on much the same terms as before our venture into the world the winter before. My father's clerkship had ended with the adjournment of the legislature in the spring, but in the autumn, when it grew toward winter, I asked again for the correspondence of the *Gazette*. I got this by favor of my friend, and then I had courage to ask for that of the Cleveland *Herald*, which the interest of the blithe sexagenarian sufficed to secure me, and I returned to the capital with no pretense that I was not now writing the letters solely and entirely myself. But almost before my labors began my health quite broke under the strain of earlier over-study and later over-work. I gave up my correspondence for both those honored newspapers to my father, who wrote it till the close of the session, and at his suggestion the letters of the *Gazette* fell the next winter to the fit and eager hands of a young man who had just then sold his country newspaper and had come to try his fortune in the capital. His name was Whitelaw Reid, in the retrospect a tall, graceful youth with an enviable black mustache and imperial, wearing his hair long in the Southern fashion, and carrying himself with the native ease which availed him in a worldly progress uninterrupted to the end. He wrote the legislative letters so acceptably that when the Civil War broke out the *Gazette* people were glad to make him their correspondent in the field, where he distinguished himself beyond any other war correspondent in the West, or the East for what I knew. The world knows how riches and honors followed him all his days, and how when he died the greatest Empire sent his dust home to the greatest Republic in such a war-ship as the war correspondent of those years could not have dreamed of. From time to time we saw each other, but not often; he was about his business in the State House, and now I was about mine in the office of the *Ohio State Journal*, the organ of the Republican party, which had been newly financed and placed on a firm footing after rather prolonged pecuniary debility.

I was at home in the autumn, as I had been all the summer, eating my heart out (as I would have said in those days) when the call to a place on the *Journal's* editorial staff incredibly, impossibly came, and I forgot my ills, and eagerly responded. I hardly know how to justify my inconsistency when I explain that this place was the same which I had rejected at twice the salary on the Cincinnati *Gazette*. Perhaps I accepted it now because I could no longer endure the disappointment and inaction of my life. Perhaps I hoped that in the smaller city the duties would not be so odious or so onerous; perhaps it was because I would have been glad to return to Columbus on any terms; in any case it fell out that the duties of the place were undertaken by another who doted on them, and quite different and far more congenial functions were assigned to me.

My chief was Henry D. Cooke, the successful editor and proprietor of a newspaper in northern Ohio, and brother of the banker Jay Cooke, once nationally noted in our finance and himself afterward Governor of the District of Columbia, the easiest of easy gentlemen, formed for prosperity and leisure, with an instinct for the choice of subordinates qualified to do the journalistic work he soon began to relinquish in his preoccupation with the politics of the capital. I have had no sweeter friend in a life abounding in friends, and after fifty years I think of his memory with gratitude for counsels which availed me much when given and would avail me still if I should ever again be a youth of twenty-one, proposing to do and say the things I then proposed. He rarely blamed anything I did in the stirring and distracted period of our relation, but one morning he brought me a too graphic paragraph, about a long-forgotten homicide done by an injured husband, and said, "Never, *never* write anything you would be ashamed to read to a woman," and so made me lastingly ashamed of what I had done, and fearful of ever doing the like again, even in writing fiction. It seems not to be so now with our novelists, begun or beginning; they write many things they ought to be ashamed to read to women, or if they are of that sex, things they should be ashamed to read to men. But perhaps they *are* ashamed and only hold out writing so for art's sake; I cannot very well speak for them; but I am still very Victorian in my preference of decency.

Mr. Cooke must have been often of a divided mind about his assistants, or about their expression of the opinions which he reticently held in common with them. He was a thorough Republican; he undoubtedly believed that the time had come for calling black black, but his nature would have been to call it dark gray, at least for that day or for the next. He would have oftenest agreed with us in what we said of the pro-slavery party and partisans, North and South, though he held it not honesty to have it thus set down. He would have liked better the *milde Macht* of a Hahnemannian treatment, while we were blistering and cauterizing, and letting blood wherever we saw the chance, and there were every day chances enough. I had been made news editor, and in the frequent intervals of our chief's abeyance I made myself the lieutenant of the keen ironical spirit who mostly wrote our leaders, but did not mind my dipping my pen in his ink when I could turn from the paste and scissors which were more strictly my means of expression. My work was to look through the exchange newspapers which flocked to us in every mail, and to choose from them any facts that could be presented to our readers as significant. I called my column or two "News and Humors of the Mail," and I tried to give it an effect of originality by recasting many of the facts, or, when I could not find a pretext for this, by offering the selected passages with applausive or derisive comment. We had French and Spanish and German exchanges, and I sometimes indulged a boyish vanity by prefacing a paragraph from these with such a sentence as, "We translate from the

Courrier des États Unis," or, "We find in *La Cronaca* of New York," or "We learn from the *Wachter am Erie,*" as the case might be. Why I should have been suffered to do this without admonition from our chief or sarcasm from my senior I do not know; perhaps the one thought it best to let youth have its head when the head was harmlessly turned; and perhaps the other was too much occupied with his own work to trouble himself with mine; but certainly if I had caught a contemporary in such folly I should have tried what unsparing burlesque could do to make him wiser.

The reader who has no follies to own will probably not think me wise in owning mine, but from time to time I must do so; there were so many. It is with no hope of repairing these follies now that I confess the pride I felt in the poor little Spanish, German, and French which it had cost me so much to acquire unaided and unguided, and I was willing that my acquirements should shed luster on the newspaper I loved almost as much as I loved myself. I admired it even more, and I wished to do all that I could to make it admirable, even enviable, with others. I think now that I was not using one of the best means to do it; I only contend that it was one of the best I could think of then. If any contemporary had turned it against us, I hope I should have been willing to suffer personally for it, but I cannot now be sure.

VI

We aspired at least tacitly to a metropolitan character in our journalism; there were no topics of human interest which we counted alien to us anywhere in the range of politics, morals, literature, or religion; and I was suffered my say. The writer who was more habitually and profitably suffered his say was, I still think, a man of very uncommon qualities and abilities. He was a journalist who could rightly be called a publicist, earnest if things came to that, of a faithful conscience and of a mocking skill in the chances pretty constantly furnished us by our contemporaries, especially some of our Southern contemporaries whom it was difficult to take as seriously as they took themselves. When they made some violent proclamation against the North, or wreaked themselves in some frenzy of pro-slavery ethics, we took our pleasure in shredding the text into small passages and tagging each of these with a note of open derision or ironical deprecation. We called it "firing the Southern heart," in a phrase much used at the time. It was not wise, it was not well, but it was undeniably amusing, and we carried it to any lengths that the very intermittent supervision of our nominal chief would allow. We may have supposed that it would help laugh away the madness of the South which few in the North believed more than a temporary insanity, but the uneasy honesty which always lurks somewhere in my heart to make me own my errors must acquit my fellow-editor of the worst excesses in this sort, so mainly literary with me. He was not only a man of high journalistic quality, of clear insight, shrewd judgment, and sincere convictions, but I do not believe that in the American press of the time he was surpassed as a clear thinker and brilliant writer. All the days of journalism are yesterdays; and the name of Samuel R. Reed will mean nothing to these oblivious morrows, even in Ohio, but all the more I wish to do his memory such honor as I may. We were of course daily together in our work, and often in our walks on the Sundays which were as other days to his steadfast agnosticism. The word was not yet, but the thing has always been, and especially it always was in the older

West, where bold surmise of the whence and whither of life often defied the authority of Faith, then much more imperative than now. Reed's favorite author, whom he read as critically as if he were not his favorite, was Shakespeare; but his far more constant reading was the Bible, especially the Old Testament. I could not say why he read it so much, but he may have felt in it the mystical power which commands the imagination of men and holds them in respectful contemplation of a self-sufficing theory of the universe such as nothing in science or philosophy affords. He quoted it for a peculiar joy in the fitness of its application to every circumstance; he quoted Dickens, as everybody did then; he quoted Shakespeare a great deal more both in his talking and in his writing; and later in his life, long after mine had parted from it, he amused the spare moments of his journalistic leisure by a study of Shakespeare's women whom he did not take at the generally accepted critical appraisement.

I am tempted out of the order of these confessions to follow him to the end which death put to the long kindness between us, and I recall with tenderness our last meeting near New York where he was hesitating whether to continue on his way to Europe. He had at last given up his work in Cincinnati where he had spent the many years after the few years we spent together in Columbus. He owned that he had worn himself out in that work, toiling incessantly through many homicidal Cincinnati summers, and he blamed himself for the sacrifice. He felt that he had turned from it too late; and in fact he died at sea soon after. He accepted his impending doom with the stoical calm which he always kept, and which I had once seen him keep so wonderfully after the war began, when a Southern Unionist, the formerly famous, now forgotten Parson Brownlow of Tennessee, came to reproach him for the part which he held that such writing as Reed's had borne in bringing on the strife. Reed suffered the good man's passion almost with compassion, and when Brownlow was gone he would not let me blame him, but said that he had played a noble part in the struggle to hold his region in the Union. He always kept a countenance of bland calm, lit by pale-blue eyes which gave no hint of the feeling within, and if I had not loved him so much and known him so well I might have thought the habitual smile of his clean-shaven lip sometimes a little cruel. He let his full soft beard grow inordinately long, and he had a way of stroking it as he slightly smiled and crisply spoke; it was the only touch of quaintness in him at a time when beards were self-indulgently worn in many fantastic ways. He was the best-dressed man I knew, in fashions as little aged as possible in their transition from the East to the West, and he was of a carefulness in such minor morals as gloves and boots very uncommon in our somewhat slovenly ways.

After his liking for Shakespeare and Dickens he liked the Ingoldsby Legends, but he did not care for the poetry which I was constantly reading and trying to write. The effect of my endeavor as it appeared in the passionate or pessimistic verse which I contributed to Eastern periodicals must have amused him; but perhaps he tolerated me because, along with this poetical effusiveness in which I was grievously sensitive to any breath of sarcasm, I had a tooth as sharp as his own in our journalism. He was intelligently and I suppose scientifically fond of music, since he failed of no chance to hear the best, a chance rare in our city; and he held that the composition of grand opera was the highest feat of the human intellect, which was to me a stumbling-block and foolishness, though I liked dramatic singing, and indeed singing of

YEARS OF MY YOUTH

all kinds. We came together in our fondness for the
theater, and after our evening's work was done he sometimes turned with me into the barnlike structure on
State Street which served the pathetic need of the drama
in Columbus at that day. The place was heated in the
winter for its twenty or thirty frequenters by two huge
cast-iron stoves, one on either side of the orchestra:
stoves such as I have since seen in English cathedrals;
but when the curtain rose the blast of freezing air that
swept out upon us made us shiver for the players in their
bare arms and necks and their thin hosiery and drapery.
They were often such bad players that they merited their
sufferings; the prompter audibly bore a very leading part
in the performance as he still does in the Italian theater;
yet for all his efforts we one night saw Hamlet in two acts;
it was, to be sure, a very cold night, of an air eagerer and
nippinger than even that the ghost walked in at Elsinore,
and we would not have had the play longer. Yet we
often saw very well given some of the old English comedies
which are now no longer well or ill given; and between
the acts, somewhere, a plain young girl, in a modest
modicum of stocking, represented the ballet by dancing
the Highland Fling, always the Highland Fling. Such
plays as "The Lady of Lyons" happened now and then,
and "The Daughter of the Regiment" must have been,
at least partly, sung. We did not lack the more darkling
melodrama, and there were heroic pieces which gave the
leading actor opportunities not lost upon him, however
they failed of effect with the rest of the cast. I remember
how one night a robustuous periwig-pated fellow ramped
and roared up and down the stage, but left quite cold a
large group of the *dramatis personæ* which his magnilo-
quence was intended to convulse with either sympathy or
antipathy; and how Reed noted with mock-thoughtful
recognition of the situation, "Can't excite those fellows

II   151

off to the left, any." I should not be able to say how killingly droll I found this.

VII

I suppose that every young man presently attempting journalism feels something of the pride and joy I felt when I began it; though pride and joy are weak words for the passion I had for the work. If my soul was more in my verse, I did not know it, and I am sure my heart was as much in my more constant labors. I could find time for poetry only in my brief noonings, and at night after the last proofs had gone to the composing-room, or I had come home from the theater or from an evening party, but the long day was a long delight to me over my desk in the room next my senior. To come upon some inviting fact, or some flattering chance for mischief in an exchange, above all a Northern contemporary with Southern principles, and to take this to him and talk it or laugh it over and leave it with him, or bring it back and exploit it myself, was something that made every day a heyday. We shunned personalities, then the stock in trade of most newspaper wits; we meant to deal only with the public character of men and things. It seems to have been all pleasure as I tell it, but there was a great deal of duty in it, too; though if burlesquing the opposite opinions of our contemporaries happened to be a duty, so much the better. If it were to do again, I should not do it, or not so much; but at the time I cannot deny that I liked doing it. So, too, I liked to write cutting criticisms of the books which it was part of my work to review; and I still hope to be forgiven by the kindness which I sinned against without winning the authority as reviewer which I aimed at.

152

I had much better been at the theater than writing
some of the things I then wrote. But it may as well
be owned here as anywhere that whatever might have
been its value to me as a school of morals the theater
was not good society in Columbus then; and I was now
in a way of being good society, and had been so for some
time. The rehabilitation of our newspaper was coincident
with the rise of the Republican party to the power which
it held almost unbroken for fifty years. It had of course
lost the Presidential election in 1856, but its defeat left it
in better case than an untimely victory might have done.
Ohio had, at any rate, a Republican Governor in a man
afterward of a prime national importance, and already
known as a statesman-like politician well fitted by capacity
and experience for that highest office which never ceased
to be his aim while he lived. Salmon P. Chase had been
a lawyer of the first standing in Cincinnati, where, although a Democrat, he had early distinguished himself
by his services in behalf of friendless negroes. The
revolt of the whole self-respecting North against the repeal
of the Missouri Compromise swept him finally out of
the Democracy into that provisional organization which
loosely knew itself as the Anti-Nebraska party; but
before he was chosen Governor by it he had already
served a term in the United States Senate, where
with one other Freesoiler he held the balance of power
in an otherwise evenly divided body. He was a large,
handsome man, of a very senatorial presence, and
now in the full possession of his uncommon powers; a
man of wealth and breeding, educated perhaps beyond
any of the other Presidential aspirants except Seward,
versed in the world, and accustomed to ease and state;
and he gave more dignity to his office, privately and
publicly, than it had yet known among us. He lived
in a pretty house of the Gothic make then much

affected by our too eclectic architecture, with his brilliant young daughter at the head of it; for the Governor was a widower.

He was naturally much interested in the new control of the Republican organ, and it would not be strange if he had taken some active part in its rehabilitation, but I do not know that he had. At any rate, he promptly made the editorial force welcome to his house, where Reed and I were asked to Thanksgiving dinner; Mr. Cooke had not yet brought his family to Columbus. Thanksgiving was not then observed on the present national terms; it was still the peculiar festival of New England, and in our capital its recognition was confined to families of New England origin; our Kentuckians and Virginians and Marylanders kept Christmas, though the custom of New-Year's calls was domesticated among us with people of all derivations, and in due time suffered the lapse which it fell into in its native New York. Our Governor was born in New Hampshire, where his family name was already distinguished in public life; and he kept the Thanksgiving which he had probably not officially invited his fellow-citizens to commemorate. I suppose we had turkey for our dinner, but I am surer of the manner than the make of the feast, for it was served with a formality new to my unworldly experience. The turkey was set before the governor who carved it, and then it was brought to the guests by a shining black butler, instead of being passed from hand to hand among them, as I had always seen it done. That was, in fact, my first dinner in society.

The young editors were the only guests; and after dinner the family did not forbid itself the gaieties befitting its young people's years. We had charades, then much affected in society, and I believe the Governor alone was not pressed into helping dramatize the riddle to be finally

guessed as Canterbury Bell. I do not remember how the
secret was kept to the end, or guessed from the successive
parts. My fear and pride were put to a crucial test in the
first dissyllable, which the girlish hostess assigned me,
and nothing but the raillery glancing through the deep
lashes of her brown eyes which were very beautiful,
could have brought me to the self-sacrifice involved.
I lived through the delight and anguish of that supreme
evening, and found myself, as it were, almost immediately
afterward in society. It could not have been quite immediately, for when I called at the Governor's soon after
New-Year's and he asked me if I had made many New-
Year's calls I answered that I had not made any because
I knew no one. Then he said I might have called at *his*
house; and I did not fail, on this kind reproach, to go to
Miss Chase's next reception, where again she laughed at
my supposed dignity in refusing to dance; she would not
suppose my inability.

But before entering that field so flowery fair which
society now seemed to open before me perhaps I had
better continue my recollections of a man whose public
career has its peculiar pathos. It was his constant, his
intense, his very just desire to be President; no man
of his long time was fitter to be President, unless his ambition was a foible that unfitted him. He accepted not
the first place, but the second place, in the administration
of the man whose place as President he had so ardently
longed to fill, and after he had resigned his governorship of
Ohio and gone to Washington as Secretary of the Treasury
under Lincoln I saw him there when I went to look after
the facts of the consulship which had been offered me.
His fellow Ohioans must have swarmed upon him in
the eagerness for public service afterward much noted
in them, and I do not blame him for imagining that I
had called upon him in the hope that he would urge

my case upon the President. He said, rather eagerly, that he had no influence with the administration (it likewise became Lincoln's own humorous complaint) quite before I had asked it, and was sorry that he could not help me; and when I thanked him and remarked that I believed the President's private secretaries, Hay and Nicolay, were interested in my affair, he said, with visible relief, Oh well, then, I was in the best possible hands; as indeed it turned out. I had heard before that he had spoken to the President in my behalf, and he may very well have felt that he had done his best.

Four years later, and ten years after my first acquaintance with Chase, I went to call upon him at his hotel in New York, when I was lately returned from my consular post in Venice, and ventured to offer him my congratulations upon his accession to the chief-justiceship of the Supreme Court. He answered bluntly that it was not the sort of office he had aspired to, and intimated that it was a defeat of his real aspirations. He was not commonly a frank man, I believe, but perhaps he felt that he could be frank with the boy I must still have seemed even at twenty-eight, bringing the devotion he possibly over-imagined in me. Since then those words of his, which were the last I was to hear from him, have been of an increasing appeal with me; and if the Republicans had not had Lincoln I still think it was a pity they could not have had Chase. At the end, the Democrats would not have him.

VIII

Chase was of course *our* man for the 1860 nomination, and the political relations between him and our chief were close; but somehow I went more to other houses than to his, though I found myself apparently launched from it upon a social tide that bore me through all the doors of the amiable little city. I was often at the evening parties (we called them evening parties then) which his daughter gave, and one day the Governor himself, as we met in the street, invited me to luncheon with him. I duly went and passed the shining butler's misgiving into the dining-room, where I found the family at table with no vacant place among them. The Governor had forgotten me! That was clear enough, but he was at once repentant, and I lunched with him, outwardly forgiving, but inwardly resolved that it should be the last time I would come at his informal bidding. I have since forgotten much more serious engagements myself; I have not gone to dinners where I have promised over my own signature to go; but at twenty-one men are proud, and I was prouder then than I can yet find any reason for having been.

In our capital at that day we had rather the social facts than the social forms. We were invited to parties ceremoniously enough, but we did not find it necessary to answer whether we would come or not. Our hostess remained in doubt of us till we came or did not come; at least that was the case with young men; we never inquired whether it was so with young girls or not. But sometimes when a certain youth wished to go with a certain maiden he found out as delicately as he could whether she was invited, and if she was he begged her to let him go with her, and arrived with her in one of the lumbering two-horse hacks which supplied our cab-service, and which I see still bulking in the far perspective of the State Street corner of the State House yard. If you had courage so high or purse so full you had sent the young lady a flower which she wore to the party, preferably a white camellia which the German florist, known to our young world only as Joe, grew very successfully, and allowed you to choose from the tree. Why preferably a camellia I could not say after this lapse of time; perhaps because its cold, odorless purity expressed the unimpassioned emotion which oftenest inspired the gift and its acceptance. It was very simple, very pastoral; I do not know when Columbus outgrew this custom, which of course it did long ago.

Bringing a young lady to a party necessarily meant nothing but that you enjoyed the pleasure of bringing her. Very likely she found her mother there when she came with you, unmindful, the one and the other, that there was such a thing as chaperonage in a more fastidious or censorious world. It seems to me, indeed, that parties at the Columbus houses were never wanting in the elders whom our American society of girls and boys used to be accused of ignoring. They superabounded at the legislative receptions, but even at the affairs which my sophistication early distinguished from those perfunctory hospitalities there were mature people enough, both married and unmarried, who, though they had felt no charge concerning their daughters or nieces, found it agreeable to remain till the young ladies were ready to be seen home by their self-chosen escorts. A youth who danced so reluctantly as I, was rather often thrown upon these charitable elders for his entertainment, and I cannot remember ever failing of it. People, and by people I do not mean women only, read a good deal in that idyllic Columbus, and it was my delight to talk with any one who would about the new books or the old. The old books were known mostly to that number of professional men— lawyers, doctors, divines, and scientists—which was disproportionately large in our capital; they were each cultivated in his own way, and in mine, too, or the better part of it, as I found. The young and the younger women read the current fiction and poetry at least enough to be asked whether they had read this thing or that; and there was a group of young men with whom I could share my sometimes aggressive interest in our favorite authors. I put the scale purposely low; I think that I could truthfully say that there was then no American community west of the Alleghanies which surpassed ours in the taste for such things. At the same time I must confess that it would be easy for such an exclusively literary spirit as I was to deceive himself, and to think that he always found what he may have oftener brought.

For a long time after the advent of our new journalism, the kind of writing which we practised—light, sarcastic, a little cruel, with a preference for the foibles of our political enemies as themes—seemed to be the pleasure of good society, which in that serious yet hopeful time did not object to such conscience as we put into our mocking. Some who possibly trembled at our boldness darklingly comforted themselves for our persiflage by the good cause in which it frisked. When anything very daring came out in the afternoon the young news-editor in his round of calls could hear the praise of it from charming readers in the evening, or he might be stopped in the street next day and told how good it was by the fathers, or brothers, or brothers-in-law, of those charming readers. It was more like the prompt acclaim the drama enjoys than the slow recognition of literature; but I, at least, was always trying to make my writing literature, and after fifty-odd years it may perhaps be safely owned that I had mainly a literary interest in the political aspects and events which I treated. I felt the ethical quality of the slavery question, and I had genuine convictions about it; but for practical politics I did not care; I wished only to understand enough of them to seize any chance for a shot at the other side which they might give. I had been in the midst of practical politics almost from my childhood; through my whole youth the din of meetings, of rallies, of conventions had been in my ears; but I was never at a meeting, a rally, or a convention; I have never yet heard a political speech to the end. For a future novelist, a realist, that was a pity, I think, but so it was.

In that day of lingering intolerance, intolerance which can scarcely be imagined in this day, and which scarcely stopped short of condemning the mild latitudinarianism of the *Autocrat of the Breakfast Table* as infidelity, every one but a few outright atheists was more or less devout. In Columbus everybody went to church; the different forms of Calvinism drew the most worshipers; our chief was decorously constant with his family at the Episcopal service; but Reed was frankly outside of all ecclesiastical allegiance, and I who, no more than he, attended any religious service, believed myself of my father's Swedenborgian faith; at any rate, I could make it my excuse for staying away from other churches, since there were none of mine. While I am about these possibly needless confidences I will own that sermons and lectures as well as speeches have mostly been wearisome to me, and that I have heard only as many of them as I must. Of the three, I prefer sermons; they interest me, they seem really to concern me; but I have been apt to get a suggestive thought from them and hide away with it in a corner of my consciousness and lose the rest. My absences under the few sermons which I then heard must have ended chiefly in the construction or the reconstruction of some scene in my fiction, or some turn of phrase in my verse.

Naturally, under these circumstances, the maturer men whom I knew were oftener doctors of medicine than

160

doctors of divinity; in fact, I do not think I knew one clergyman. This was not because I was oftener sick than sorry; I was often sorry enough, and very sensible of my sins, though I took no established means of repenting them; but I have always found the conversation of physicians more interesting than that of most other men, even authors. I have known myself in times past to say that they were the saints of the earth, as far as we then had saints, but that was in the later Victorian period when people allowed themselves to say anything in honor of science. Now it is already different; we have begun to have our doubts of doubt and to believe that there is much more in faith than we once did; and I, within the present year, my seventy-ninth, have begun to go to church and to follow the sermon with much greater, or more unbroken, attention than I once could, perhaps because I no longer think so much in the terms of fiction or meditate the muse as I much more used to do.

In those far days I thought prose fit mainly for everyday use in newspaper work. I was already beginning to print my verses in such of the honored Eastern periodicals as would take them: usually for nothing. I wrote for the *Saturday Press* of New York, which ambitious youth everywhere were then eager to write for, and I wrote for the *Atlantic Monthly* oftener than I printed in it. I have told all this and more in *My Literary Passions* and I will not dwell here upon the whirl of æsthetic emotion in which I eddied round and round at that tumultuous period. In that book I have also sufficiently told the story of my first formal venture in the little volume of verse which I united with my friend John J. Piatt in offering to the world. But I may add here that it appeared just at Christmas-time in 1859 from the press of a hopeful young publisher of Columbus who was making his experiment in the disquieting hour when no good thing was expected to come out of our Western Nazareth. We two were of the only four poets west of the Alleghanies who had yet been accepted by the *Atlantic*, and our publisher had the courage to make our book very pretty in print and binding. It was so pretty that I am afraid some readers liked it for its looks; one young lady said that I at least could have no trouble in choosing what Christmas presents I should make my friends. She was that very beautiful girl who easily bore the palm for beauty in Columbus, and I do not yet understand how I was able to reject her unprofessional suggestion with as much pride as if she had been plain. I gave my book to no one, in my haughty aversion from even the shadow of advertising, and most of my friends had their revenge, I suppose, in not buying it.

IX

I had begun now to know socially and intrinsically the little capital which I had known only politically and extrinsically during the two winters passed there as a legislative correspondent. I then consorted with the strangers whom their share in the government made sojourners, and who had little or no local quality to distinguish them from one another. I shared the generalized hospitalities offered them with that instinctive misgiving which I have rather more than hinted; and though I distinguished among them, and liked and valued certain of them, yet I had a painful sense of our common exteriorality and impermanence. I cannot say that I ever expected to become part of the proper life of the city, and when suddenly I found myself in that life, if not of it, I was very willing to find it charming. How charming it was compared with the life of other cities I had no means of knowing, but now after the experiences, not too exhaustive, of half a century I still feel it to have been charming, with the wilding grace proper to all the West in those days, and the refinement remembered from the varied culture (such culture as there was) of the East and South it derived from.

Not so many people in our town could have known me for my poetry as for my journalism, and I do not pretend that the sexes were equally divided in their recognition. I have intimated my fancy that with most men, men of affairs, men of the more serious callings, the face of the poet was saved by the audacity of the paragrapher. If I could be so sharp, so hard in my comment on the day's events, I could not be so soft as I seemed in those rhymes where I studied the manner of Heine, the manner of Tennyson, and posed in this or that dramatized personality. I cannot flatter myself that I did not seem odd sometimes to many of my fellow-citizens, though I hope that with some of the hardest-headed among them I was acceptable for qualities which recommend average men to one another. Some of that sort made friends with me; some even who were of an entirely diverse political thinking tolerated my mockeries of opinions which they supposed their principles. But neither my pleasure nor my pride was in such friendships. What I wished to do always and evermore was to think and dream and talk literature, and literature only, whether in its form of prose or of verse, in fiction, or poetry, or criticism. I held it a higher happiness to stop at a street corner with a congenial young lawyer and enter upon a fond discussion of, say, De Quincey's essays than to prove myself worthy the respect of any most eminent citizen who knew not or loved not De Quincey. But I held it far the highest happiness to call at some house where there were young girls waiting and willing to be called upon and to join them in asking and saying whether we had read this or that late novel or current serial. It is as if we did nothing then but read late novels and current serials, which it was essential for us to know one another's minds upon down to the instant; other things might wait, but these things were pressing.

Of course there were some houses where such problems were of more immediate and persistent interest than other houses. Such a house was the ever-dear house of the S. family, which made itself a home any hour of the day up to midnight for such youth as had once been adopted its sons. It was not only a literary house, it was even more a musical house, where there was both singing and playing, with interludes of laughing and joking in all forms of seemly mirth, with the whole family, till the little boys of it stumbled up the stairs half asleep. I could not play, but I was sometimes suffered by that large-hearted hospitality to try singing; and I could talk with the best. So, it was my more than content in the lapses of the music to sit with the young aunt (she seemed so mature in her later twenties to me in my earliest) and exchange impressions of the books new and old that we had been reading. We frequenters of the house held her in that honor which is the best thing in the world for young men to feel for some gentle and cultivated woman; I suppose she was a charming person apart from her literary opinions; but we did not think of her looks; we thought of her wise and just words, her pure and clear mind.

It was the high noon of Tennyson and Thackeray and George Eliot and Dickens and Charles Reade, whose books seemed following one another so rapidly. *The Newcomes* was passing as a serial through *Harper's Magazine,* and we were reading that with perhaps more pleasure than any of the other novels and with the self-satisfaction in our pleasure which I have before this argued was Thackeray's most insidious effect with youth striving to spurn the world it longed to shine in. We went about trying to think who in the story was like whom in life, and our kind hostess was reading it, too, and trying to think that, too; but it was not well for her to say what she thought in the case of the handsomest, and for several reasons, really, the first among us. It appeared that she thought he was like Clive Newcome and that we others were like those friends of his whom in the tale his nature was shown subordinating. She said something like this to some one, and when her saying came to us others we revolted in a body. No, we would not have that theory of our relation to our friend; and I do not know to what infuriate excess of not calling for a week we carried our resentment. I do not know how after the week, if it was so long, we began calling again; but I surmise it was through something said or done by that dear Miss A. which made it easy for her sister to modify her wounding theory into a recognition of the proud equality which bound us friends together.

We are all dead now, all save me and· the youngest daughter of the house, but as I think back we are all living again, and others are living who are also dead. Among these is a young lady visitor from a neighboring city, one of those beautiful creatures who render the Madonna faces of the painters credible, and of a prompt gaiety which shared our wonted mirth in its own spirit. Her beauty might have dedicated her to any mysterious fate; beauty is often of such tragical affinition; but not her gaiety; and yet the glad die, too, and this glad creature within a year had gone to the doom which sent no whisper back to the hearts left lifelong aching. Her father was appointed consul to a Mediterranean port, and she sailed with him in the ship which sailed with them both into eternity, unseen, unsignaled, as messageless as if it had been a mist swept from the face of the sea.

But well a year before this time and a year after our first meeting in Columbus I saw her in Boston, in a house swept as wholly from the face of the earth as that ship from the face of the sea. I suppose the Court House in Boston is an edifice as substantial as it is plain, but for me, when I look at the place where it stands my vision pierces to the row of quiet, dignified mansions which once lined that side of Somerset Street, and in one of which I somehow knew that I should find with her uncle's family the beautiful creature already so unimaginably devoted to tragedy, to mystery, to the eternal baffle of surmise. It seemed that from often being there she knew the city so enchanted and enchanting to me then, and she went about with me from one wonder of it to another; and it remains in the glimmer of that association, which no after-custom could wholly eclipse. It was a moment of the glad young American life of other days which seems so impossible to after days and generations; and with the Common and its then uncaterpillared elms, with the Public Garden, just beginning in leaf and flower, with the stately dwellings which looked upon those pleasances in the streets long since abandoned to business, with the Public Library, the fine old Hancock House, and the Capitol as Bullfinch designed and left it, and the Athenæum as it used to be, and Faneuil Hall, swarming with memories for my young ardor, and the Old State House, unvisited by its manifold transformations,—the brave little city of the past is all contemporaneous again.

X

As I have said, all they of that Columbus house but one are gone. One of the little boys went before they were men, and then the other; the mother went long afterward; the elder daughter, who had been the widow of our repudiated Clive Newcome, went longer afterward yet; and then still later, finding myself once on a very mistaken lecturing-tour in Kansas, where our beloved Miss A. had lived many married years, I asked for her, hoping to see her, and heard that she had died the year before. But first of all the father died, leaving me the memory of kindness which I hardly know how to touch aright. He was my physician as well as my friend, and saw me through the many maladies, real and unreal, of my ailing adolescence, but he would have no fee for curing me of either my pains or my fears. I had come to him first with my father, who somehow knew him before me, and it was as if he became another father to me. Often in those nights of singing and playing, of talking and joking, he would look in for a moment between patients to befriend our jollity; and when at last it came to my leaving Columbus, and going that far journey to Venice, whither I seemed bound as on a journey to another planet, he asked me one night into his little outside office by the State Street gate, and had me tell him what provision I had made for the chances before me. I told him, and then whether he thought it not enough in that war-time when the personal risks were doubled by the national risks he said, "Well, I am not a rich man, or the son of a rich man, but if you think you need something more, I can let you have it." I had been keeping my misgivings to myself, but now I owned them and borrowed the two hundred dollars which he seemed to have there with him, as if in expectation of my need.

For a darker tint in the picture I have been painting of my past let me record here a fact which may commend itself for the younger reader's admonition; the old cannot profit by it, perhaps, though as long as we live we are in danger of forgetting kindness. When my family first came to Columbus we were much beholden to another family, poor like ourselves, which did everything but turn itself out of doors to let us have the little house we were to occupy after them. They shared it with us till they could place themselves elsewhere; and my father and mother remained bound to them in willing gratitude. When I came back to the capital after my five years of exile in our village I, too, remembered our common debt, but when the world began to smile upon me I forgot the friends who had not forgotten me till one day my father wished me to go with him to see them. The mother of the family received me with a sort of ironical surprise, and then her hurt getting the better, or the worse, of her irony, she said some things about my losing sight of humble friends in the perspectives opening so alluringly before me. I could not recall, if I would, just the things she said, but they scorched, and the place burns yet; and if I could go back and repair the neglect which she brought home to me how willingly, after nearly sixty years, would I do it! But at the time I hardened my heart and as I came away I tried to have my father say something in extenuation of the fault which I angrily tried to make a merit of; but with all his tenderness for me he would not or could not.

Perhaps he, too, thought that I had been a snob, a thing that I had not needed the instruction of Thackeray to teach me the nature of; but I hope I was not so bad as that; I hope there was nothing meaner in me than youth flattered out of remembrance of old kindness by the new kindness in which it basked. I will confess here that I have always loved the world and the pleasures which other sages pretend are so vapid. If I could make society over, or make it over a little, so that it would be inclusive rather than exclusive, I believe I would still like to go into it, supposing it always sent a motor to fetch and carry me and did not insist upon any sort of personal exertion from me. But when I was between twenty and twenty-three and lived in Columbus I was willing to be at almost any trouble for it. All up and down the wide shady streets which ran from High eastward, and were called Rich and Town and State and Broad, there were large pleasant houses of brick, with or without limestone facings, standing in lawns more ample or less, and showing through their trees the thrilling light of evening parties that burst with the music of dancing from every window. Or if this was not the case with every house, beautiful girls were waiting in every other to be called upon, beside the grates with their fires of soft coal, which no more discriminated between winter and summer than the dooryard trees which seem to have been full-foliaged the whole year round.

It may be that with the passage of time there began to be shadows in the picture otherwise too bright. It seems to me that in time the calls and balls may have begun to pall and a subtle *Weltschmerz*, such as we had then, to pierce the heart; but scarcely any sense of that remains. What is certain is that the shadow of incredible disaster which was soon to fill the whole heaven still lurked below the horizon, or if it showed itself there, took the form of retreating clouds which we had but to keep on laughing and singing in order to smile altogether out of sight. The slavery question which was not yet formidably a question of disunion was with most of the older men a question of politics, though with men like Dr. S. it was a question of ethics; with the younger men

169

it was a partisan question, a difference between Democrats and Republicans; with me it was a question of emotions, of impassioned preoccupations, and in my newspaper work a question of copy, of material for joking, for firing the Southern heart. It might be brought home to us in some enforcement of the Fugitive Slave Law, as in the case of the mother who killed her children in Cincinnati rather than let them be taken back with her to Kentucky; or in the return of an escaping slave seized in our own railroad station; and there was at first the horror of revolted humanity and then the acquiescence of sickened patience. It was the law, it was the law; and the law was constitutional and must be obeyed till it was repealed. Looking back now to that law-abiding submission, I can see that it was fine in its way, and I can see something pathetic in it as well as in the whole attitude of our people, the South and North confronted in that inexorable labyrinth, neither side quite meaning it or realizing it.

That was a very crucial moment indeed, but the crisis had come for us five or six years before when the case of some conscientious citizens, arrested in the Western Reserve for violation of that abominable law, came before Chief-Justice Swann of the Ohio Supreme Court. It was hoped by the great majority of the Republican party and largely expected that Justice Swann's opinion would in whatever sort justify the offenders, and it was known that the Governor would support the decision with an armed force against the United States, which must logically attempt the execution of the law with their troops. Very probably the state of Ohio would have been beaten in such an event, but Justice Swann defeated the popular hope and expectation beforehand by confirming the judgment against those right-minded but wrong-headed friends of humanity. Ohio was spared the disaster which befell South Carolina five or six years later, and Justice Swann suffered the penalty of men whose judgment is different from the convictions of their contemporaries. From being one of the most honored leaders of his party, with the prospect of any highest place in its gift, he remained one of the most distinguished jurists of his time whose best reward came coldly from those who would not blame where they could not praise. In Ohio the judiciary is elective, and Judge Swann hastened the decision of the court before the meeting of the Republican State Convention in order that his party might not unwittingly renominate him in the expectation of an opinion from him favorable to the good men of Ohio who had broken the bad law of the United States.

There is a legend, cherished more for its dramatic possibility than for any intrinsic probability, that when Lincoln appointed Noah L. Swayne justice of the Supreme Court of the United States he supposed that he was appointing Joseph Swann, and that he was misled by the similarity of the names, not very great either to ear or eye. Swayne was then one of the most eminent members of the Columbus bar, and, though he lacked the judicial experience of Swann, was entirely fit for the place he was called to fill. If such a mistake was made it was one which could well retrieve itself, but it seems a very idle fancy which has toyed with its occurrence. It would be altogether too nice in the face of its unlikelihood to inquire whether Lincoln might have wished to express a certain sympathy for the eminent jurist in the arrest of his public career which followed his decision. One would first have to establish the fact of such a feeling in him and prove that if he had it he would have been so careless of the jurist's name as to mistake another name for it. These are the things that happen in fiction when the

171

novelist is hard driven by the exigencies of his plot, but cannot easily occur in sober history.

I met both of these prominent men during my Columbus years, as an improminent young fellow-citizen might, Justice Swayne rather often, and Justice Swann once at least, in their own houses. On this sole occasion, which dimly remains with me, I was paying one of those evening calls which we youth were diligent in making at houses where there were young ladies; and after due introduction to the great jurist, I was aware of him, withdrawn and darkling in the next room, not unkindly, but not sensibly contributing to the gaiety of the time in me. That might have been after I was asked to a party at his house, which I was told, by a lady versed in such mysteries, was the greatest distinction which society had to offer in our city, and I suppose from this fact that the popular blame for his momentous decision, even if it was of much force, did not follow him into more rarefied air.

XI

We young men of that time were mostly Republicans, but some of us were Democrats and some of us were Southerners, or derivatively Southern. I have said how little society with us was affected by New England, even in such a custom as Thanksgiving, and I may go a little farther and say how it was characterized for good as well as for evil by the nearer South rather than the farther East, but more for good than for evil. Many people of Southern origin among us had chosen a Northern home because they would rather live in a Free State than a Slave State; they had not cast their sectional patriotism, but when it came to a question of which ideal should prevail, they preferred the Northern ideal. They derived from that South which antedated the invention of the cotton-gin, and which could take a leading part in keeping the Northwestern Territory free, with Ohio the first Free State born of that great mother of Free States. The younger generation of their blood were native Ohioans, and these were not distinguishable from the children of the New-Englanders and the Scotch-Irish Pennsylvanians by anything that I can remember. We had already begun to be Ohioans, with an accent of our own, and I suppose our manners were simpler and freer than those of the East, but the American manners were then everywhere simple and free, and are so yet, I believe, among ninety-nine hundred-thousandths of our ninety-nine millions. It seems to me now that the manners in Columbus were very good then among the young people. No one can say what change the over-muchness of subsequent money may have made in them, but one likes to think the change, if any, is not for the better. There seems to have been greater pecuniary equality then than there is now; there was an evener sky-line, with scarcely a sky-scraping millionaire breaking it anywhere. Within what was recognized as society there was as much social as pecuniary equality; apparently one met the same people everywhere on that easily ascertained level above the people who worked for their living with their hands. These were excluded, as they always have been excluded from society in all times and places; so that if I had still been a compositor at the printer's case I could not have been received at any of the houses that welcomed me as a journalist, though that did not occur to me then, and only just now occurs to me, as something strange and sad; something that forever belies our democracy, but is so fast and deep-rooted in the conditions which our plutocracy has kept from our ancestral monarchies and oligarchies and must keep as long as men live upon one another in the law of competition.

In one house there was more singing and playing and in another more reading and talking. All the young ladies were beautiful, with the supremacy of that young lady whom it was our poetry to hold so beautiful that no other might contest it. As I believe the use still is in the South, we called them Miss Lilly, Miss Julia, Miss Sally, Miss Fanny, Miss Maggie, whether they were the older or the younger daughters of the family. We were always meeting them at parties or, failing that or including that, we went to call upon them at their houses. We called in the evening and it was no strange thing for a young man to call every evening of the week, not at one house, but at three or four. How, in the swift sequence of the parties, we managed so often to find the young ladies at home remains one of the mysteries which age must leave youth to solve. Possibly in that sharply foreshortened perspective of the past the parties show of closer succession than they really were.

At most of the houses we saw only the young ladies; it was they whom we asked for; but there were other houses where the mothers of the family received with the daughters, and at one of these my welcome was immediately of a kindness and always of a conscience which it touches me to realize. I was taken at the best I meant as well as the best I was by the friend who was the exquisite spirit of the house, and made me at home in it. My world had been very small, and it has never since been the greatest, but I think yet, as I divined then, that she was of a social genius which would have made her in any great-worldlier capital the leader she was in ours, where her supremacy in that sort was no more questioned than the incomparable loveliness of that most beautiful girl whom every one worshiped. Her house expressed her, so that when her home finally changed to another the new house obeyed the magic of her taste and put on the semblance of the first, with a conservatory breathing through it the odor of her flowers and the murmur of the dove that lived among them: herself a flower-like and birdlike presence, delicate, elegant, such as might have been fancied of some fine, old-world condition in a new-world reading of it. She lived to rule socially in a community which attested its gentleness by its allegiance to her until she was past eighty, but when I knew her first she was too young to be titularly accepted as their mother by her stepdaughters and was known to them as their cousin in what must have been her own convention; but I suppose she liked to be not less than sovereign among her equals. With me she was not only the kindest, but the most candid of my friends; my literary journalism and later my literature may have been to her liking, but she never flattered me for them when, as I now know, too much praise had made me hungry for flattery. No young man such as I was then could have had a wiser and faithfuler friend, and I render her memory my tribute after so many years from a gratitude which cannot be spoken. After so many years I cannot make out whether she accepted or merely suffered my extreme opinions in politics; though she was wholly Ohioan, her husband's family had close affiliations with the South; but hers was certainly a Republican house, as nearly all the houses I frequented were. What may have made her even anticipatively my friend was our common acceptance of the Swedenborgian philosophy, which long, long afterward, the last time I saw her, I spoke of as a philosophy. But then she rejected the notion with scorn; it might be a pleasant fancy, she said, but a philosophy, no; and I perceived that she had come the way of that agnosticism which the whole cultivated world had taken. Now I have heard that in her last years she went back to the faith which was perhaps more inherited than reasoned in both of us. But I am sure that it was at first a bond and that she was conscientiously true to this bond of a common spiritual tradition, when upon some public recognition of my work she reminded me how according to Swedenborg every beautiful thing we said or did was by an influx from the divine. I submitted outwardly, but inwardly I rebelled: not that my conceit of the things I did was so very great; I believe I thought rather modestly of myself for doing them, and I always meant to do much better things; in fact I still have my masterpiece before me; but, poor things as they were, I wished to feel them wholly mine.

For a kindred reason I quite as altogether refused, and more explicitly, the theory of my old friend, Moncure D. Conway, as to the true function of the West in literature. He was then a young Unitarian minister, preaching at Cincinnati an ever-widening liberalism in religion, and publishing a slight monthly magazine named after *The Dial* of Emerson at Concord, and too carefully studied from it. For this paler avatar of that transcendental messenger he had asked me for contributions, and so a friendship, which lasted throughout our lives, sprang up between us. When he once came to Columbus he came to lunch with me, and quite took my appetite away by propounding his theory that the West was to live its literature, especially its poetry, rather than write it, the East being still in that darkling period when it could not live its literature. I do not remember the arguments by which he supported his thesis; but proofs as of holy writ could not have persuaded me of it as far as I myself was concerned. My affair was to make poetry, let who would live it, and to make myself known by both the quality and quantity of my poetry. It is not clear to me now how I declared my position without immodesty, but somehow I declared it, and so finally that Conway was very willing to carry away with him for his magazine a piece of rhyme which I had last made. He could the more willingly do this because *The Dial* was one of those periodicals, commoner then than now, that paid rather in glory than in money; in fact it was not expected to pay anything in money, so that I doubly defeated him: I was not only not living my poetry, I was not even living by it.

IV

THE days of the years when youth is finding its way into manhood are not those which have the most flattering memories. It is better with the autobiographer both before and after that time, though both the earlier and later times have much to offer that should keep him modest. But that interval is a space of blind struggle, relieved by moments of rest and shot with gleams of light, when the youth, if he is fortunate, gathers some inspiration for a worthier future. His experiences are vivid and so burnt into him that if he comes to speak of them it will require all his art to hide from himself that he has little to remember which he would not much rather forget. In his own behalf, or to his honor and glory, he cannot recall the whole of his past, but if he is honest enough to intimate some of its facts he may be able to serve a later generation. His reminiscences even in that case must be a tissue of egotism, and he will merit nothing from their altruistic effect.

I

Journalism was not my ideal, but it was my passion, and I was passionately a journalist well after I began author. I tried to make my newspaper work literary, to give it form and distinction, and it seems to me that I did not always try in vain, but I had also the instinct of actuality, of trying to make my poetry speak for its time and place. For the most part, I really made it speak for the times and places I had read of; but while Lowell was keeping my

Heinesque verses among the *Atlantic* MSS. until he could make sure that they were not translations from Heine I was working at a piece of realism which when he printed it in the magazine our exchange newspapers lavishly reprinted. In that ingenuous time the copyright law hung loosely upon the journalistic consciousness and it was thought a friendly thing to reproduce whatever pleased the editorial fancy in the periodicals which would now frowningly forbid it, but with less wisdom than they then allowed it, as I think. I know that as its author the currency of *The Pilot's Story* in our exchanges gave me a joy which I tried to hide from my senior in the next room; and I bore heroically the hurt I felt when some of the country papers printed my long, overrunning hexameters as prose. I had studied the verse not alone in Longfellow's "Evangeline," but in Kingsley's "Andromeda," and Goethe's "Hermann and Dorothea," while my story I had taken from a potentiality of our own life, and in the tragedy of the slave girl whose master gambles her away at *monte* on a Mississippi steamboat, and who flings herself into the river, I was at home with circumstance and scenery. I still do not think the thing was ill done, though now when I read it (I do not read it often) I long to bring it closer to the gait and speech of life. The popularity of the piece had its pains as well as pleasures, but the sharpest anguish I suffered was from an elocutionist who was proposing to recite it on the platform, and who came to me with it to have me hear him read it. He did not give it with the music of my inner sense, but I praised him as well as I could till he came to the point where the slave girl accuses her master with the cry of—

"Sold me! Sold me! Sold! And you promised to give me
    my freedom!"

179

when he said, "And here I think I will introduce a shriek."
"A shriek?" I faltered. "Yes, don't you think it would
fill the suspense that comes at the last word 'Sold!'?
Something like this," and he gave a screech that made my
blood run cold, not from the sensibility of the auditor,
but the agony of the author. "Oh no!" I implored him,
and he really seemed to imagine my suffering. He
promised to spare me, but whether he had the self-denial
to do so I never had the courage to inquire.

In the letters to my sister which I was so often writing
in those Columbus years I find record of the constant
literary strivings which the reader shall find moving or
amusing as he will. "I have sold to Smith of the Odd
Fellow's Monthly at Cincinnati that little story I read to
you early last summer. I called it 'Not a Love Story.'
He gave me six dollars for it; and he says that as soon
as I have time to dress up that translation which B.
rejected he will buy that. At the rate of two dollars a
page it will bring me sixteen or eighteen dollars. 'Bobby'"
—I suppose some sketch—"is going the rounds of the
country papers. The bookseller here told our local editor
that it was enough to make anybody's reputation—that
he and his family laughed prodigiously over it. . . . I
have the assurance that I shall succeed, but at times I
tremble lest something should happen to destroy my
hopes. I think, though, that my adversity came first,
and now it is prosperity lies before me. I am going to
try a poem fit to be printed in the *Atlantic*. They pay
Fullerton twenty-five dollars a page. I can sell, now,
just as much as I will write."

It was two years yet before that poem I was trying
for the *Atlantic* was fit, and sold to the magazine for
twenty-five dollars, though it was three pages long. I
was glad of the pay, but the gain was nothing to the glory;
and with the letter which Lowell wrote me about it in the

pocket next my heart, and felt for to make sure of its presence every night and morning and throughout the day, I was of the potentiality of immeasurable success. I should have been glad of earning more money, for there were certain things I wished to do for those at home which I could not do on my salary of ten dollars a week, already beginning to be fitfully paid. Once, I find that I had not the money for the white gloves which it seems I expected myself to wear in compliance with usage at a certain party; and there were always questions of clothes. Dress-coats were not requisite then and there; the young men wore frock-coats for the evening, but I had ambitiously provided myself with the other sort upon the example of a friend who wore his all day; I wore mine outdoors once by day, and then presciently dedicated it to evening calls. The women dressed beautifully, to my fond young taste; they floated in airy hoops; they wore Spanish hats with drooping feathers in them, and were as silken balloons walking in the streets where men were apt to go in unblacked boots and sloven coats and trousers. The West has, of course, brushed up since, but in that easy-going day the Western man did not much trouble himself with new fashions or new clothes.

II

Whether the currency of *The Pilot's Story* and the *Atlantic* publication of my Heinesque poems added to my reputation in our city I could not say. It was the belief of my senior on the newspaper that our local recognition was enervating and that it had better go no farther, but naturally I could not agree with a man of his greater age and observation, and it is still a question with me whether recognition hurts when one has done one's best. I cannot recall that I ever tried to invite it; I hope not; but certainly I worked for it and hoped for it, and I doubt if any like experiment was ever received with more generous favor than ours by a community which I had reasons for knowing was intelligent if not critical. Our paper, if I may say it, was always good society, but after a while and inevitably it became an old story, or at least an older story than at first, though it never quite ceased to be good society. There remained the literary interest, the æsthetic interest for me, after the journalistic interest had waned; there was always the occasion, or the occasion could always be made. Passages in those old letters home remind me that we talked long and late about *The Marble Faun* one night at a certain house; at another we talked about other books from nine o'clock on, I imagine till midnight. At another the young lady of the house "sang about a hundred songs." At still another the girl hostess said, "You haven't asked me to sing to-night, but I will sing," and then sang divinely half the night away, for all I know. There was a young lady who liked German poetry, and could talk about Goethe's lyrics; and apparently everywhere there were the talking and the laughing and the singing which fill the world with bliss for youth.

Perhaps I sacrifice myself in vain by my effort to impart the sense of that past which faded so long ago; perhaps some readers will hold me cheap for the fondness which recurs to it and lingers in it. But I believe that I prize its memories because they seem so full of honor and worship for the girlhood and womanhood which consecrate it in my remembrance. Within this gross world of ours as it now is, women are still so conditioned that they can lead the life of another and a better world, and if they shall ever come to take their rightful share of the government of the world as men have made it I believe they will bring that other and better world of

182

theirs with them and indefinitely advance the millennium.
I have the feeling of something like treason to the men
I knew in that time, when I own that I preferred the
society of women to theirs, but I console myself with the
reflection that they would probably have said the same
as to mine. Our companionship could hardly have
chosen itself more to my liking. It was mainly of law
students, but there was here and there one engaged in
business, who was of a like joking and laughing with the
rest. We lived together in a picturesque edifice, Gothic
and Tudor, which had been meant for a medical college,
and had begun so, and then from some financial infirmity
lapsed to a boarding-house for such young men as I knew,
though we were not without the presence of a young
married pair, now and then, and even a young lady, a
teacher or the like, who made us welcome when we ended
a round of evening calls outside by calling on them from
room to room. In my boyhood days at Columbus I was
sometimes hustled off the sidewalk by the medical students coming from the College, then in its first prosperity, and taking up the whole pavement as they swept
forward with interlinked arms. This was at noontime,
when they were scarcely less formidable than the specters
which after dark swarmed from the dissecting-room, and
challenged the boy to a trial of speed in escaping them.
Now the students had long been gone from the College
and I dwelt in its precincts with such other favorites of
fortune as could afford to pay three dollars and a half
a week for their board. The table was even super-
abundant, and the lodging was almost flatteringly comfortable after experience of other places. I can only
conjecture that the rooms we inhabited had been meant
for the students or professors when the College was still
a medical college. They were large, and to my untutored
eye, at least, were handsome, and romantically lighted by

windows of that blend of Tudor and Gothic which I have mentioned, but their architecture showed more on the outside than on the inside, and of course the pinnacles and towers of the edifice were more accessible to the eye without. It was the distinction of people who wished to be known for a correct taste to laugh at the architecture of the College, and perhaps they do so still, but I was never of these. For me it had, and it has, a charm which I think must have come from something like genius, if not quite genius, in the architect, to whose daring I would like to offer this belated praise. At any rate it was the abode of entire satisfaction to me in those happy years between 1857 and 1860 when I could not have wished other companionship than I had there.

There could have been no gayer table than we kept, where we made the most of one another's jokes, and were richly personal in them, as youth always is. The management was of the simplest, but not incompatible with dignity, for the landlord waited upon the table himself, and whoever the cook might be, the place was otherwise in the sole charge of an elderly maid, with a curious defect of speech, which kept her from answering, immediately or ultimately, any question or remark addressed to her. We valued her for this impediment because of the pathetic legend attaching to it, and we did not value her the less, but the more, because she was tall and lank and uncouth of face and figure, though of a beauty in her absolute faithfulness to her duties and the kindness beyond them which she always showed. The legend was that in her younger if not fairer time she had been married, and when one day her husband, suddenly killed in an accident, was brought home to her, she tried to speak, but could not speak, and then ever afterward could only speak after great stress, and must often fall dumb, and go away without speaking.

I do not know whether we really believed in this or not, but we behaved as if we did, and revered the silent heroine of the tragedy as if it were unquestionably true. What kept me from trying to make it into a poem I cannot say, but I would like to think it was that I felt it above rather than below the verse of even the poet I meant to be. How many rooms she had charge of I could as little say, but I am certain that there were two of us young men in each of them. My own room-mate was a poet, even more actual than myself, though not meaning so much as I to be always a poet; he was reading law, and he meant to practise it, but he had contributed two poems to the *Atlantic Monthly* before any of mine had been printed there. This might have been a cause of bitterness with me; his work was certainly good enough to be a cause of bitterness, and perhaps I was not jealous because I felt that it would be useless; I should like to believe I was not even jealous of him for being so largely in society before I was. Later, when we came in from our evening calls, we sometimes read to each other, out of what books I could not say now, but probably some poet's; certainly not our own verse: he was too wise for that and I too shy.

He was then reading law, and sometime in my middle years at Columbus he left us to begin his law practice farther West. In noticing his departure as a friendly journalist should I obeyed his wish not to speak of him as a poet; that, he said, would injure him with his new public; but whether it would or not I am not sure; the Western community is sometimes curiously romantic, and does not undervalue a man for being out of the common in that way. What really happened with him was that, being of a missionary family and of a clerical tradition, he left the law in no great time and studied divinity. It was a whole generation afterward before I saw him again;

185

and now his yellow hair and auburn beard of the early days were all one white, but his gentle eyes were of the old hazel, undimmed by the age that was creeping upon us both. He had followed me with generous remembrance and just criticism in my fiction; and again he made me a sort of professional reproach for dealing in my novels (notably in *A Modern Instance*) with ethical questions best left to the church, he thought. I thought he was wrong, but I am not sure that I so strenuously think so now; fiction has to tell a tale as well as evolve a moral, and either the character or the principle must suffer in that adjustment which life alone can effectively manage. I do not say ideally manage, for many of the adjustments of life seem to me cruel and mistaken. If it is in these cases that religion can best intervene, I suppose my old friend was right; at any rate, he knows now better than I, for he is where there is no manner of doubt, and I am still where there is every manner of doubt.

I believe, in the clerical foreshadowing of his future, perhaps, he was never of those wilder moments of our young companionship when we roamed the night under the summer moon, or when we forgathered around the table in a booth at the chief restaurant, and over a spirit-lamp stewed the oysters larger and more delicious than any to be found now in the sea; or when in the quarter-hours of digestion which we allowed ourselves after our one-o'clock dinner we stretched ourselves on the grass, often sunburnt brown, before the College and laughed the time away at anything which pretended itself a joke.

We collegians were mostly Republicans as most of the people we knew were. A few young men in society were not, but they were not of our companionship, though we met them at the houses we frequented, and did not think the worse of them for being Democrats. In fact, there was no political rancor outside of the newspapers, and that was tempered with jocosity. Slavery had been since the beginning of the nation, the heritage of the states from the colonies, and it had been accepted as part of the order of things. We supposed that sometime, somehow, we should be rid of it, but we were not sanguine that it would be soon; and with so many things of pressing interest, the daily cares, the daily pleasures, the new books, the singing and laughing and talking in the pleasant houses, I could leave the question of slavery in abeyance, except as a matter of paragraphing. There had been as many warnings of calamity to come as ever a people had. There had been the breaking of solemn promises from the South to the North; there had been the bloody fights between the sections in Kansas and the treacheries of the national government; there had been the quarrels and insults and violences in Congress; there had been the arrests and rescues of fugitive slaves; there had been the growth of hostile opinion, on one side fierce and on the other hard, maturing on both sides in open hate. There had been all these portents, and yet when the bolt burst from the stormy sky and fell at Harper's Ferry we were as utterly amazed as if it had fallen from a heaven all blue.

III

Only those who lived in that time can know the feeling which filled the hearts of those who beheld in John Brown the agent of the divine purpose of destroying slavery. Men are no longer so sure of God's hand in their affairs as they once were, but I think we are surer that He does not authorize evil that good may come, and that we can well believe the murders which Brown did as an act of

187

war in Kansas had not His sanction. In the mad skurry
which followed the incident of Harper's Ferry in 1859
some things were easily shuffled out of sight. Probably
very few of those who applauded or palliated Brown's
attempt knew that he had taken men from their wives
and children and made his partisans chop them down
that their death might strike terror into the pro-slavery
invaders, while he forbore from some strange policy to
slaughter them with his own hand. His record was not
searched to this dreadful fact in my knowledge, either
by the Democrats who tried to inculpate the Republicans
for his invasion of Virginia or by the Republicans who
more or less disowned him. What his best friends could
say and what most of them believed, was that he had been
maddened by the murder of his sons in Kansas, and
that his wild attempt was traceable to the wrongs he had
suffered. His own dignity as he lay wounded and cap-
tive in the engine-house at Harper's Ferry, where the
volunteer counsel for the prosecution flocked upon him
from every quarter, and questioned him and cross-
questioned him, did the rest, and a sort of cult grew up
which venerated him before his death. I myself was
of that cult, as certain fervent verses would testify if
I here refused to do so. They were not such very bad
verses, as verses, though they were technically faulty in
places, but in the light which Mr. Oswald Villard's history
of John Brown has finally cast upon that lurid passage
of his life I perceive that they were mistaken. He was
not bloodier than most heroes, but he was not a martyr,
except as he was willing to sacrifice himself along with
others for a holy cause, and he was a saint only of the
Old Testament sort of Samuel who hewed Agag in pieces
before the Lord. But from first to last he was of the
inevitable, and the Virginians could no more have saved
themselves from putting him to death than he could

have saved himself from venturing his life to free their slaves.   Out of that business it seems to me now that they came with greater honor than their Northern friends and allies.   The South has enough wrongs against the negroes to answer for in the past and in the present, but we cannot lay wholly to its charge the fate of the slave's champion; he was of the make of its own sons in his appeal to violence, and apparently the South understood him better than the North.   There was then no evil too great for us to think or say of the Virginians, and yet after they could free him from the politicians, mainly Northern, who infested him in the first days of his captivity, to make political capital or newspaper copy out of him, the Virginians tried him fairly, as those unfair things called trials go, and they remained with a sort of respect for him which probably puzzled them.   Long after, twenty-five years after, when I was in an ancient Virginia capital it was my privilege to meet some of Governor Wise's family; and I noted in them this sort of retrospective respect for Brown; they were now of Republican politics, and I found that I was not nearly Black Republican enough for them.   But in the closing months of the year 1859 there was no man so abhorred and execrated by the so-called Black Republicans as Governor Wise.

Without going to the files of our own newspaper I cannot now say just how we treated the Harper's Ferry incident from first to last, but I am safe in saying that it was according to the temperament of each writer. Our chief, who wrote very well when he could detach his interest from the practical politics so absorbing in the capital of a state like Ohio, may have struck the key-note of our opinion in an able leader, and then left each of us to follow with such music as responded in us.   My vague remembrance of the result is the daily succession of most penetrating, most amusing comments from my senior. The event offered him the opportunity of his life for that cold irony he excelled in and which he knew how to use so effectively in behalf of a good cause; I do not believe it was ever employed in a bad one. The main contribution to the literature of the event from his junior that I can distinctly recall was that ode or that hymn to John Brown, for which I cannot yet be ashamed or sorry, however I must rue the facts that have forever spoilt my rapture in it. I have the sense of a pretty constant passing from the room where I was studying the exchanges for material, and trying to get my senior's laugh for something I had written, or staying for him to read me the article he had just begun or finished. It was a great time, though it was a dreadful time, so thick with forecast, if we had only known it, of the dreadfuler time to follow.

While I have been saying this I have been trying to think how much or little our community was shaken by an event that shows so tremendous in the retrospect, and it seems to me little rather than much. People knew the event was tremendous, but so had the battles in Kansas been, and so had the attack on Sumner in the Senate Chamber, and so had the arrests and rescues of the fugitive slaves. They were of the same texture, the same web which fate was weaving about us and holding us faster, hour by hour and day by day while we felt ourselves as free as ever. There must have been talk pretty constant at first, but dying away without having really been violent talk, among people who differed most about it. What I think is that most people were perhaps bewildered, and that waiting in their daze they did not say so much as people would now imagine their saying. Or it may be that my memory of the effect is a blur of so many impressions that it is impossible to

190

detach any from the mass; but I do not think this probable. The fact probably is that people did not realize what had happened because they could not, because their long experience of enmity between the South and North had dulled them too much for a true sense of what had happened.

But I wrote home to my father my disappointment that his paper had not had something "violent" about the John Brown raid. My head, which abstractly passionate and concretely descriptive rhymes had once had wholly to themselves, was now filled with John Brown when it could be relieved of a news-editor's duty; I thought of him and him only, except when I was making those perpetual calls at those pleasant houses where the young ladies were singing or talking every night. I got some consolation from one of the delightful German editors whom I seemed to know in those days. He was a '48 man, and he carried in his leg a ball which some soldier of the king had planted there one day when my friend stood behind a barricade in Berlin. He told me, as I read in one of my old letters home, that he had been teaching his children the stories of Schiller, the good poet of freedom, of Robert Blum, the martyr of liberty, and of our John Brown. He says, "My liddle girl, ven I deached dem to her, she veeped."

But I cannot recall having spoken of Brown with my friend Dr. S., whom I was so apt to speak with of the changing aspects of the slavery question, though I remember very well his coldness to my enthusiasm for the young English poet, Richard Realf, who was so grotesquely Secretary of State in the Republic Brown had dreamed out, but who had passed from Canada with his department before the incident at Harper's Ferry, and was in Texas at the time of it and of the immediately ensuing events. What affair of state brought him to Columbus after the death of his leader and comrades I did not understand, and I cannot understand yet how he could safely be there within easy reach of any United States marshal, but he was, no doubt, much safer there than in Texas, and he stayed some days, mainly talking with me about himself as a poet rather than as a Secretary of State. He interested me, indeed, much more as a poet, for I already knew him as the author of some Kansas war lyrics, which I am not sure I should admire so much now as I did then. He was a charming youth, perhaps my senior by two years, and so about twenty-four, gentle mannered, sweet voiced, well dressed, and girlishly beautiful. I knew, as he was prompt and willing to tell me again, that he had been a protégé of Lady Byron's, and that while in her house he had fallen in love with a young kinswoman of hers, and was forced to leave it, for with all his gifts he was the son of an agricultural laborer, and for that reason no desirable match. Yet Lady Byron seemed to have remained fond of him; she had helped him to publish a volume of verse which he had called *Guesses at the Beautiful* (I envied him the title), and at parting she had given him a watch for a keepsake and money to bring him to America. He showed me the watch, and I dare say the volume of poems, but I am not sure as to this, and I vouch for no particular of his story, which may very well have been wholly true. In the long walks and long talks we had together, when he cared more to speak of his literary than his military life, I cannot make out that he expected to help further in any attack upon the South. Apparently he shared the bewilderment which every one was in, but he did not seem to be afraid or anxious for himself as part of the scheme that had so bloodily failed. He was not keeping himself secret, and he went on to Canada as safely as he had come from Texas, if indeed he went to Canada.

While he was briefly with us a hapless girl, of those whom there is no hope for in this life, killed herself, and Realf went to the wicked house where she lay dead, out of some useless pathos, since she *was* dead. I reported the fact to my friend Dr. S. with a faltering tendency, I am afraid, to admire Realf for it, and the doctor said, coldly, Yes, he had better kept away; his motive had already been scandalously construed. It was this world speaking at its best and wisest, but I am not sure that it altogether persuaded me.

IV

Realf's stay in Columbus must have been in that time of abeyance between Brown's capture and his death; but it must have been after the hanging at Charlestown that one night I was a particle of the crowd which seemed to fill the State House yard on its western front, dimly listening to the man whose figure was a blur against the pale stone. I knew that this man was that Abraham Lincoln who had met Stephen A. Douglas in the famous Illinois debates, and who was now on his way home to Illinois from his recognition in the East as a man of national importance. I could not well hear what he said, and I did not stay long; if I had heard perfectly, I might not, with my small pleasure in public speaking, have stayed long; and of that incident, and of the man whom history had already taken into her keeping, and tragedy was waiting to devote to eternal remembrance, I have only the vision of his figure against the pale stone, and the black crowd spread vaguely before him. Later I had a fuller sense of his historic quality, but still so slight, when he stood on the great stairway within the State House and received the never-ending crowd which pushed upward, man and woman after man and woman, and took his hand, and tried to say something as fit as it was fond. That would have been when he was on the journey, which became a flight, to his inauguration as President at Washington. He had been elected President, and the North felt safe in his keeping, though the dangers that threatened the nation had only gathered denser upon it, and the strange anomaly which called itself the government had been constantly betraying itself to the hostility within it and without.

The people who pushed upward to seize the great hand held out to every one looked mostly like the country folk such as he had been of, and the best of him always was, and I could hear their hoarse or cracked voices as they hailed him, oftenest in affectionate joking, sometimes in fervent blessing; but for anything I could make out he answered nothing. He stood passive, submissive, with the harsh lines of his lower face set immovably, and his thick-lashed eyes sad above them, while he took the hands held up to him one after another, and shook them wearily, wearily. It was a warm day such as in late February, or earliest March, brings the summer up to southern Ohio before its time, and brings the birds with it for the delusion of a week or a fortnight; and as we walked out, my companion and I, we left a sweltering crowd within the State House, and, straying slowly homeward, suffered under a sun as hot as June's.

v

I do not say July's sun or August's, because I wish my reader to believe me, and any one who has known the July or August, or the September even, of southern Ohio has known something worse than tropical heat, if travelers tell the truth of the tropics; and no one could believe me if I said such heat ever came in February or March.

There were whole fortnights of unbroken summer heat in Columbus, when the night scarcely brought relief from the day, and the swarming fly ceded, as Dante says, only to the swarming mosquito. Few people, even of those who might have gone, went away; none went away for the season, as the use is now, though it is still much more the use in the East than in the West. There were excursions to the northern lakes or to Niagara and down the St. Lawrence; there were even brief intervals of resort to Cape May; but the custom was for people to stay at home, to wear the thinnest clothes, and drink cooling drinks, and use fans, and try to sleep under mosquito-bars, after sitting out on the front steps. That was where calls were oftenest paid and received, and as long as one was young the talk did not languish, though how one did when one was old, that is, thirty or forty, or along there, we who were young could not have imagined. There was no sea or any great water to send its cooling breath over the land which stretched from the Ohio River to Lake Erie with scarcely a heave of its vast level. We had not even the satisfaction of knowing that we were suffering from a heat-wave; the notion had not been invented by quarter of a century yet; we suffered ignorantly on and on, and did not intermit our occupations or our pleasures; some of us did not even carry umbrellas against the sun; these we reserved for the rain which could alone save us, for a few hours in a sudden dash, or for a day in the storm that washed the air clean of its heat.

The deluging which our streets got from these tempests was the only cleaning which I can recollect seeing them given. There was indeed a chain-gang which intermittently hoed about in the gutters, but could not be said to clean them, while it remained the opprobrium of our civilization. It was made up mostly of negroes, but there were some drink-sodden whites who dragged a lengthening chain over the dust or hung the heavy ball which each wore over the hollows of their arms when urged to more rapid movement. Once I saw, with a peculiar sense of our common infamy in the sight, a quite well-dressed young man, shackled with the rest and hiding his face as best he could with eyes fastened on the ground as he scraped it. Somehow it was told me that he had been unjustly sentenced to this penalty, and the vision of his tragedy remains with me yet, as if I had acted his part in it. I dare say it was not an uncommon experience by which when I used to see some dreadful thing, or something disgracefully foolish, I became the chief actor in the spectacle; at least I am certain that I suffered with that hapless wretch as cruelly as if I had been in his place. Perhaps we are always meant to put ourselves in the place of those who are put, or who put themselves, to shame.

Municipal hygiene was then in its infantile, if not in its embryonic stage, and if there was any system of drainage in Columbus it must have been surface drainage, such as I saw in Baltimore twenty-five years later. After the rain the sun would begin again its daily round from east to west in a cloudless sky where by night the moon seemed to reflect its heat as well as its light. They must still have such summers in Columbus, and no doubt the greatest part of the people fight or faint through them as they do in our cities everywhere, but in those summers even the good people, people good in the social sense, remained, and not merely the bad people who justly endured hardship because of their poverty. I had become accustomed to the more temperate climate of the Lake Shore, and I felt the heat as something like a personal grievance, but not the less I kept at work and kept at play like the rest. Once only I was offered the chance

196

of escape for a few days (it was in the John Brown year of 1859) when I was commissioned to celebrate the attractions of a summer resort which had been opened a few hours away from the capital. I had heard much talk of the coolness of White Sulphur, as it was called, and I expected much more than I had heard, but I now got much more than I had expected.

There must have been a break in the heat when at some unearthly hour of the July morning I had taken the train which would leave me at White Sulphur, but in the sleep which youth can almost always fall into I was not sensible of it. I say fell into, but I slept upright as one did on the trains in those times, and when my train stopped at the station which as yet made no sign of being a station I stumbled down the car steps to a world white with frost in the July morning. My foot slid over the new planking of the platform as on ice, and on the way up to the new hotel the fences bristled with the glacial particles which bearded the limbs of the wayside trees, and the stubble of the wheat and fields, and the blades of the corn, and sparkled in the red of the early sun which was rising to complete the devastation. I was in those thinnest summer linens, with no provision of change against such an incredible caprice of the weather, and when I reached the hotel there was no fire I could go to from the fresh, clean, thrillingly cold chamber, with its white walls and green lattice door, which I was shown into. No detail of the time remains with me except what now seems to have been my day-long effort to keep warm by playing ninepins with a Cincinnati journalist, much my senior, but as helpless as myself against the cold. There must have been breakfast and dinner and supper, with their momentary heat, but when I went to bed I found only the lightest summer provision of sheet and coverlet, and I was too meek to ask for blankets.

VI

What account I gave of the experience in print I cannot say after the lapse of fifty-seven years, but no doubt I tried to make merry over it, with endeavor for the picturesque and dramatic. Through the whole of a life which I do not complain of for lasting so long, though I do not like being old, I have found that in my experiences, where everything was novel, some of the worst things were the things I would not have missed. It had not been strictly in the line of my duty as news editor to make that excursion, but I dare say I did it gladly, for the reasons suggested. There were other reasons which were to make themselves apparent during the year: on my salary of ten dollars a week I could not afford to be very punctilious; and if I was suffered to stray into the leading columns of the editorial page I could not stand upon the dignity of the news editor if I was now and then invited to do a reporter's work. Besides, there were tremors of insecurity in my position, such as came from the bookkeeper's difficulty in sometimes finding the money for my weekly wage, which might well have alarmed me for the continued working of the economic machine. Like every man who depends upon the will or power of another man to give him work, I served a master, and though I served the kindest master in the world, I could not help sharing his risks. It appeared that our newspaper had not been re-established upon a foundation so firm but that it needed new capital to prop it, after something over a year, and then a business change took place which left me out. I was not altogether sorry, for about the same time my senior resigned and went to Cincinnati to cast in his fortunes as joint owner and editor with another paper. Without him, though I should have fearlessly undertaken the entire conduct of our journal, I should not have felt so much at home in it, for I did not know then, as I have learned and said long since, that a strong writer, when he leaves a newspaper, leaves a subtle force behind him which keeps him indefinitely present in it. But there was no question of my staying, and though my chief's wish to have me stay almost made it seem as if I were staying, I had to go, and I had to leave him my debtor in two hundred dollars. I hasten to say that the debt was fully paid in no very long time, but it seems to me that the world was managed much less on a cash basis in those days than in these; people did not expect to be paid their money as soon as they had earned it; the economic machine creaked and wabbled oftener, and had to be sprinkled with cool patience when the joints worked dry of oil. This may be my fancy, partly built from the fact that my father in his life of hard work was nearly lifelong in debt, while others lived and died as many dollars in debt to him.

It must have been before this humiliating event, which I cannot exactly date, that I was asked to deliver the poem before the Ohio Editorial Convention which used annually to grace its meeting with some expression in verse. There must have been an opening prayer and an address, but I remember neither of these, and I should not be able to remember my poem, or any part of it, if it had not afterward been printed in our newspaper, from which the kindness of a friend has rescued it for me. I have just read it over, not wholly with contempt, but not without compassion for those other editors who listened to it and could have followed its proud vaticinations but darkly. It appears that I then trusted the promises of a journalistic future which have not all been kept as yet, and that I cast my prophecies in a form and mood which I might have accused Tennyson of imitating if he had not been first with his "In Memoriam."

The Men that make the vanished past
  So brave, the present time so base,
  And people, with their glorious race,
The golden future, far and vast!—

All ages have been dark to these,
  The true Knights Errant! who have done
  Their high achievements not alone
In the remoter centuries;

But ever to their dawn's dim eye,
  Blinded with night-long sorcery,
  Warring with Shadows seemed to be,—
In victory, seemed to fall and die!

Noons glowed. The poet held each name
  In hushless music to the ear—
  Low for the thinking few to hear,
Loud for the noisy world's acclaim;

And pondering, one that turns the page
  Whereon their story hath been writ,
  Gathers a purer lore from it,
Than all the wisdom of the sage;—

A simple lore of trust and faith
  For Life's fierce days of dust and heat,—
  To keep the heart of boyhood sweet
Through every passion, unto death—

To love and reverence his time,
  Not for its surface-growth of weeds,
  But for its goodly buried seeds,—
To hope, and weave a hopeful rhyme!

The vision does not seem very clear even to me, now,
and I suppose not many of those kind, hard-working
country printers and busy city journalists recognized
themselves in my forecast of the coming newspaper man.

Yet I think there is something in the glowing fancy which is here reflected only in part, and I believe some graduate of our university courses of journalism may possibly do worse than keep my fond dream in mind. In this case, the yawning counting-room may not so soon engulf his high intentions, and, keeping clear of that shining sepulcher of noble ideals for a while, he may thank me for my over-generous faith in him.

No one that I can recall specifically thanked me at the time of that editorial convention, though no doubt the usual resolutions thanking the orator and poet were passed. I should be glad to believe that at the ball which crowned our festival some kind woman-soul may have tried to feign a pleasure in my verse which no man-soul attempted; but I have only the memory of my fearful joy in the dance which I seem to have led. I went back to Columbus with such heart as I could, but in the dense foreshortening of the time's events I cannot find that of my own unhorsing from the shining procession of journalists figured in my poem. I can only be sure that I *was* unhorsed, and then suddenly, to my great joy and even greater surprise, was caught up and given a new mount, with even larger pay. That is, I was now invited to become professional reader for the young publisher who had issued the *Poems of Two Friends*, and who, apparently inspired by the signal failure of that book, imagined establishing a general publishing business in our capital. He followed it with several very creditable books, and he seems to have had the offer of many more manuscripts than he could handle. I have no doubt I dealt faithfully with these, and I know that he confided entirely in my judgment, for I was now twenty-three, without a doubt of my own as to my competence. There was one manuscript, offered by a lady who had lived some years in Chile, which I thought so

201

interesting, though so formless, that I wrote it quite over, and my friend published it in a book which I should like to read again; but I have no hope of ever seeing it. He also published a very good Ohio version of Gautier's *Romance of a Mummy*, but our bravest venture was a book which the publisher himself had fancied doing, and which he had fancied my writing. This was the life of Abraham Lincoln, printed with his speeches in the same volume with the life and speeches of Hannibal Hamlin, who was nominated with him on the Presidential ticket at the Republican Convention in 1860. It was the expectation of my friend, the very just and reasonable expectation, that I should go to Springfield, Illinois, and gather the material for the work from Lincoln himself, and from his friends and neighbors. But this part of the project was distasteful to me, was impossible; I felt that there was nothing of the interviewer in me, at a time when the interviewer was not yet known by name even to himself. Not the most prophetic soul of the time, not the wisest observer of events, could have divined my loss; and I was no seer. I would not go, and I missed the greatest chance of my life in its kind, though I am not sure I was wholly wrong, for I might not have been equal to that chance; I might not have seemed to the man whom I would not go to see, the person to report him to the world in a campaign life. What we did was to commission a young law student of those I knew, to go to Springfield and get the material for me. When he brought it back, a sheaf of very admirable notes, but by no means great in quantity, I felt the charm of the material; the wild poetry of its reality was not unknown to me; I was at home with it, for I had known the belated backwoods of a certain region in Ohio; I had almost lived the pioneer life; and I wrote the little book with none of the reluctance I felt from studying its sources.

I will not pretend that I had any prescience of the greatness, the tragical immortality, that underlay the few
simple, mostly humble, facts brought to my hand. Those
who see that unique historic figure in the retrospect
will easily blame my youthful blindness, but those who
only knew his life before he overtopped all the history
of his time will not be so ready to censure me for my
want of forecast. As it was, I felt the inadequacy of
my work, and I regretted it in the preface which owned
its hasty performance.

There were several campaign lives of Lincoln which
must have seemed better than mine to him; I cannot care
now how it seemed to others; but what he thought of it
I never knew. Within a few years I have heard that he
annotated a copy of it, and that this copy is still somewhere extant in the West; but I am not certain that I
should like to see it, much as my curiosity is concerning
it. He might, he must, have said some things which
could not console me for missing that great chance of my
life when I was too young to know it. I saw him twice
in Columbus, as I have told here already, and once in
Washington, as I have told elsewhere. That was when
I came from the office of his private secretaries at the
White House, secure of my appointment as Consul at
Venice, and lingered wistfully as he crossed my way
through the corridor. Within no very long time past
my old friend Piatt (he of the *Poems of Two Friends*) has
told me that Lincoln then meant me to speak to him,
as I might very fitly have done, in thanking him for my
appointment, and that he had followed me out from the
secretaries' room to let me do so. He might have had
some faint promptings of curiosity concerning the queer
youth who had written that life of him from material
which he would not come to him for in person. But
without doubting my friend, I doubt the fact; neither

Hay nor Nicolay ever mentioned the matter to me in our many talks of Lincoln; and I cannot flatter myself that I missed another greatest chance of my life. Rather, I imagine that he did not know who I was, or could in the least care, under the burdens which then weighed upon him. He might have suspected me an office-seeker without the courage to approach him instead of the office-seeker whose hopes he had, very likely without vividly realizing it, crowned with joy. I blame myself for not speaking to him, of course, as I blame myself for not having gone to him instead of sending to him for the facts of his past; in any event, with my literary sense, I must have valued those facts; but if Lincoln had not been elected in 1860 he would not have been nominated again; and in that case should I now be reproaching myself so bitterly?

VII

Another fame so akin to Lincoln's in tragedy, and most worthy of mention in the story of his great time, is that of a state senator of ours in the legislative session of 1860. James A. Garfield, of whose coming to read Tennyson to us one morning in the *Journal* office I have told in *My Literary Passions*, was then a very handsome young man of thirty, with a full-bearded handsome face, and a rich voice suited to reading "The Poet" in a way to win even reluctant editors from their work to listen. It is strange that I should have no recollection of meeting Garfield again in Columbus, or anywhere, indeed, until nearly ten years later, when I stopped with my father over a night at his house in Hiram, Ohio, where we found him at home from Congress for the summer. I was then living in Cambridge, in the fullness of my content with my literary circumstance, and as we were sitting with the Garfield family on the veranda that overlooked their lawn I was beginning to speak of the famous poets I knew when Garfield stopped me with "Just a minute!" He ran down into the grassy space, first to one fence and then to the other at the sides, and waved a wild arm of invitation to the neighbors who were also sitting on their back porches. "Come over here!" he shouted. "He's telling about Holmes, and Longfellow, and Lowell, and Whittier!" and at his bidding dim forms began to mount the fences and follow him up to his veranda. "Now go on!" he called to me, when we were all seated, and I went on, while the whippoorwills whirred and whistled round, and the hours drew toward midnight. The neighbors must have been professors in the Eclectic Institute of Hiram where Garfield himself had once taught the ancient languages and literature; and I do not see how a sweeter homage could have been paid to the great renowns I was chanting so eagerly, and I still think it a pity my poets could not have somehow eavesdropped that beautiful devotion. Under the spell of those inarticulate voices the talk sank away from letters and the men of them and began to be the expression of intimate and mystical experience; and I remember Garfield's telling how in the cool of a summer evening, such as this night had deepened from, he came with his command into a valley of the Kanawha; for he had quickly turned from laws to arms, and this was in the beginning of the great war. He said that he noticed a number of men lying on the dewy meadow in different shapes of sleep, and for an instant, in the inveterate association of peace, he thought they were resting there after the fatigue of a long day's march. Suddenly it broke upon him that they were dead, and that they had been killed in the skirmish which had left the Unionist force victors. Then, he said, at the sight of these dead men whom other men had killed, something went out of him,

205

the habit of his lifetime, that never came back again: the sense of the sacredness of life, and the impossibility of destroying it. He let a silence follow on his solemn words, and in the leading of his confession he went on to say how the sense of the sacredness of other things of peace had gone out of some of the soldiers and never come back again. What was not their own could be made their own by the act of taking it; and he said we would all be surprised to know how often the property of others had been treated after the war as if it were the property of public enemies by the simple-hearted fellows who had carried the use of war in the enemy's country back into their own. "You would be surprised," he ended, "to know how many of those old soldiers, who fought bravely and lived according to the traditions of military necessity, are now in the penitentiary for horse-stealing."

Once again I memorably met Garfield in my father's house in Ashtabula County (the strong heart of his most Republican Congressional district) where he had come to see me about some passages in Lamon's *Life of Lincoln*, which was then in the hands of my Boston publishers, withheld in their doubt of the wisdom or propriety of including them. I think Garfield was then somewhat tempted by the dramatic effect these passages would have with the public, but he was not strenuous about it, and he yielded whatever authority he might have had in the matter to the misgiving of the publishers; in fact, I do not believe that if it had been left to him altogether he would have advised their appearance. I met him for the last time in 1879 (when my wife and I were for a week the guests of President Hayes), as he was coming, with Mrs. Garfield on his arm, from calling upon us at the White House. He stopped me and said, "I was thinking how much like your father you carried yourself," and I knew that he spoke from the affection which had been many years between them. I was yet too young to feel the resemblance, but how often in my later years I have felt and seen it! As we draw nearer to the door between this world and the next it is as if those who went before us returned to us out of it to claim us part of them.

VIII

I never had any report of the book's sales, but I believe my *Life of Lincoln* sold very well in the West, though in the East it was forestalled by the books of writers better known. In the quiet which followed with a business which is always tending to quiescence (if the mood of the trade when discouraging authors may be trusted) my young publisher suggested my taking one hundred and seventy-five dollars of my money, and going to Canada and New England and New York on a sort of roving commission for another work he had imagined. It was to be a subscription book reporting the state and describing the operation of the principal manufacturing industries, and he thought it an enterprise peculiarly suited to my powers. I did not think so, but I was eager to see the world, especially the world of Boston, and I gladly took my hundred and seventy-five dollars and started, intending to do my best for the enterprise, though inwardly abhorring it. The best I could do was to try seeing the inner working of an iron foundry in Portland, where I was suspected of designs upon the proprietorial processes and refused admission; and I made no attempt to surprise the secrets of other manufacturers. But I saw Niagara Falls, which did not withhold its glories from me in fear of the publicity which I gave them in my letters to the Cincinnati *Gazette;* and

I saw the St. Lawrence River and Montreal and Quebec, with the *habitant* villages round about them. I also saw the ocean at Portland (not so jealous of its mysteries as the iron foundry); I saw Boston and Cambridge, and Lowell and Holmes, and their publisher, Fields; I saw New York and Walt Whitman and the Hudson River. This has been fully told in my *Literary Friends and Acquaintance,* and need not be told again here; but what may be fittingly set down is that when I arrived home in Columbus I found the publishing business still quieter than I had left it, and my friend with no enterprise in hand which I could help him bring to a successful or even unsuccessful issue. In fact he had nothing for me to do in that hour of mounting political excitement, and this did not surprise me. Neither did it surprise me that my old chief of the *State Journal* should ask me to rejoin him, though it did greatly rejoice me. He was yet in that kind illusion of his that he was working too hard on the paper; he expressed his fear that in the demand made upon his time by public affairs he should not be able to give it the attention he would like, and he proposed that I should return to a wider field in it, on an increased wage; he also intimated that he should now be able to bring up my arrears of salary, and he quite presently did so.

Again I was at the work which I was always so happy in, and I found myself associated in it on equal terms with a man much nearer my own age than my former associate Reed was. My new fellow-journalist had come to our chief from his own region in northwestern Ohio; I do not know but from his old newspaper there. I cannot write the name of Samuel Price without emotion, so much did I rejoice in our relation to the paper and each other, with its daily incident and bizarre excitement throughout the year we were together. I like to bring

his looks before me; his long face with its deep, vertical
lines beside the mouth, his black hair and eyes and smoky
complexion; his air very grave mostly, but with an
eager readiness to break into laughter. It seems to me
now that our functions were not very sharply distinguished, though I must have had charge as before of the
literary side of the work. We both wrote leading editorials, which our chief supervised and censored for a while
and then let go as we wrote them, perhaps finding no
great mischief in them. Reed remained the tradition
of the office, and if I had formed myself somewhat on his
mood and manner, Price now formed himself on mine;
and somehow we carried the paper through the year
without dishonor or disaster.

It was that year so memorable to me for having five
poems published in the *Atlantic Monthly*, two of them
in the same number, and I must have been strongly
confirmed in my purpose of being a poet. Of course I
knew too much of the world, and the literary world,
to imagine that I could at once make a living by poetry,
but I probably expected to live by some other work until
my volumes of poetry should accumulate in sufficient
number and sell in sufficient quantity to support me
without the aid of prose. As yet I had no expectation of
writing fiction; I had not recovered from the all-but-
mortal blow dealt my hopes in the failure of that story
which I had begun printing in my father's newspaper
before I had imagined an ending for it, though I must
for several years have been working in stolen moments
at another story of village life, which I vainly offered to
the *Atlantic Monthly* and the *Knickerbocker Magazine*,
and after that for many years tried to get some publisher
to bring out as a book. The manuscript must still somewhere exist, and I should not be surprised, if I ever found
it, to find myself respecting it for a certain helpless

reality in its dealing with the conditions I knew best when I began writing it. But it was still to be nearly ten years before I tried anything else of the sort, and even in *Their Wedding Journey*, which was my next attempt, I helped myself out with travel-adventure in carrying forward a slender thread of narrative. Every now and then, however, I wrote some sketch or study, which I printed in our newspaper, where also I printed pieces of verse, too careless or too slight to be hopefully offered for publication in the East.

IX

I was not only again at congenial work, but I was in the place that I loved best in the world, though as well as I can now visualize the town which had so great charm for me then I can find little beauty in it. High Street was the only street of commerce except for a few shops that had strayed down from it into Town Street, and the buildings which housed the commerce were not impressive, and certainly not beautiful. A few hotels, three or four, broke the line of stores; there was the famous restaurant of Ambos, and some Jewish clothiers; but above all, besides a music and picture store, there was an excellent bookstore, where I supplied myself from a good stock of German books, with Heine and Schiller and Uhland, and where one could find all the new publications. The streets of dwellings stretched from High Street to the right, over a practically interminable plain, and shorter streets on the left dropped to the banks of the Scioto where a lower level emulated the inoffensive unpicturesqueness of the other plain. A dusty bridge crossed the river, where in the slack-water ordinarily drowsed a flock of canal-boats which came and went on the Ohio Canal. Some old-fashioned, dignified dwellings stood at the northern end of High Street, with the country close beyond, but the houses which I chiefly knew were on those other streets. I cannot say now whether they added to the beauty of the avenues or not; I suppose that oftenest they did not embellish them architecturally, though they were set in wide grounds among pleasant lawns and gardens. The young caller knew best their parlors in winter and their porches in summer; there was little or no lunching or dining for any one except as a guest of pot-luck; and the provisioning was mainly, if not wholly, from the great public market. Greengrocers' and butchers' shops there were none, but that public market was of a sumptuous variety and abundance, as I can testify from a visit paid it with a householding friend who drove to it in his carriage, terribly long before breakfast, and provisioned himself among the other fathers and the mothers who thronged the place with their market-baskets. This was years after my last years in Columbus, when I was a passing guest; while I lived there I was citizen of a world that knew no such household cares 'or joys.

On my return from my travels, though I was so glad to be again in Columbus, I no longer gave myself up to society with such abandon as before. I kept mostly to those two houses where I was most intimate, and in my greater devotion to literature I omitted to make the calls which were necessary to keep one in society even in a place so unexacting as our capital. Somewhat to my surprise, somewhat more to my pain, I found that society knew how to make reprisals for such neglect; I heard of parties which I was not asked to, and though I might not have gone to them, I suffered from not being asked. Only in one case did I regret my loss very keenly, and that was at a house where Lincoln's young private secretaries, Hay and Nicolay, passing through to Washington before the inauguration, had asked for me. They knew of me as the author of "The Pilot's Story" and my other poems in the *Atlantic Monthly*, as well as that campaign life of Lincoln which I should not have prided myself on so much; but I had been justly ignored by the hostess in her invitations, and they asked in vain. I fully shared after the fact any disappointment they may have felt, but I doubt if I was afterward more constant in my social duties; I was intending more and more to devote myself to poetry, and with a hand freer than ever, if that were possible, in the newspaper, I was again feeling the charm of journalism, and was giving to it the nights which I used to give to calls and parties.

I did not go back to live in the College, but with Price I took a room and furnished it; we went together for our meals to the different restaurants, a sort of life more conformable to my notion of the life of the literary freelance in New York. But let not the reader suppose from this large way of speaking that there were many restaurants in Columbus, or much choice in them. The best, the only really good one, was that of Ambos in High Street, where, as I have said before, we silvern youth resorted sometimes for the midnight oyster, which in handsome half-dozens was brought us on chafingdishes, to be stewed over spirit-lamps and flavored according to our taste with milk and butter. We cooked them for ourselves, but our rejected, or protested, Clive Newcome was the most skilled in an oyster stew, and we all emulated him as we sat at the marble table in one of the booths at the side of the room. In hot weather a claret punch sometimes crowned the night with a fearful joy, and there was something more than bacchanalian in having it brought with pieces of ice clucking in a pitcher borne by the mystical Antoine from the bar where he had mixed it: that Antoine whom we romanced as of strange experiences and recondite qualities, because he was of such impregnable silence, in his white apron, with his face white above it, damp with a perennial perspiration, which even in the hottest weather did not quite gather into drops. We each attempted stories of him, and somewhere yet I have among my manuscripts of that time a very affected study done in the spirit and manner of the last author I had been reading.

I suppose he was not really of any intrinsic interest, but if he had been of the greatest I could not have afforded, even on my increased salary, to resort to Ambos's for frequent observation of him. Ambos's was the luxury of high occasions, and Price and I went rather for our daily fare to the place of an Americanized German near our office, where the cooking was very good, and the food without stint in every variety, but where the management was of such an easy kind that the rats could sometimes be seen clambering over the wall of the storeroom beyond where we sat. There was not then the present feeling against those animals, which were respected as useful scavengers, and we were rather amused than revolted by them, being really still boys with boys' love of bizarre and ugly things. Once we had for our guest in that place the unique genius destined to so great fame as Artemus Ward; he shared our interest in the rats, and we joked away the time at a lunch of riotous abundance; I should say superabundance if we had found it too much. For a while also we ate at the house of a lady who set a table faultless to our taste, but imagined that the right way to eat pie was with a knife, and never gave a fork with it. Here for a while we had the company of the young *Cincinnati Gazette* correspondent, Whitelaw .Reid, joyful like ourselves under the cloud gathering over our happy world. One day, after the cloud had passed away in the thunder and lightning of the four years' Civil War, he came radiant to my little house at Cambridge with a piece of news which I found it as difficult to realize for fact in my sympathy with him as he could have wished. "Just think! Horace Greeley has asked me to be managing editor of the *Tribune*, and he offers me six thousand dollars a year!" A great many years afterward we met in a train coming from Boston to New York, when he brought the talk round to the Spanish War, and, for whatever reason, to his part in the Treaty of Paris and the purchase of the Philippines. "*I* did that," he said. But I could not congratulate him upon this as I did upon his coming to the editorship of the *Tribune*, being of a different mind about the acquisition of the Philippines.

X

Sometime during that winter of 1860–61 Greeley himself paid us a visit in the *Journal* office and volunteered a lecture on our misconduct of the paper, which he found the cause of its often infirmity. We listened with the inward disrespect which youth feels for the uninvited censure of age, but with the outward patience due the famous journalist (of such dim fame already!) sitting on the corner of a table, with his soft hat and his long white coat on, and his quaint child-face, spectacled and framed in long white hair. He was not the imposing figure which one sees him in history, a man of large, rambling ambitions, but generous ideals, and of a final disappointment so tragical that it must devote him to a reverence which success could never have won him. I do not know what errand he was on in Columbus; very likely it was some political mission; but it was something to us that he had read the *Journal*, even with disapproval, and we did not dispute his judgments; if we were a little abashed

214

by them we hardened our hearts against them, whatever they were, and kept on as before, for our consciences were as clear as our hearts were light. No one at that time really knew what to think or say, the wisest lived from day to day under the gathering cloud, which somehow they expected to break as other clouds in our history had broken; when the worst threatened we expected the best.

Price was not the companion of my walks so much as Reed had been; he was probably of frailer health than I noticed, for he died a few years later; and I had oftener the company of a young man who interested me more intensely. This was the great sculptor, J. Q. A. Ward, who had come to the capital of his native state in the hope of a legislative commission for a statue of Simon Kenton. It was a hope rather than a scheme, but we were near enough to the pioneer period for the members to be moved by the sight of the old Indian Fighter in his hunting-shirt and squirrel-skin cap, whom every Ohio boy had heard of, and Ward was provisionally given a handsome room with a good light, in the State House, where he modeled I no longer know what figures, and perhaps an enlargement of his "Kenton." There I used to visit him, trying to imagine something of art, then a world so wholly strange to me, and talking about New York and the æsthetic life of the metropolis. My hopes did not rise so high as Boston, but I thought if I were ever unhorsed again I might·find myself on my feet in New York, though I felt keenly the difference between the places, greater then than now, when literary endeavor is diffused and equally commercialized everywhere. Ward seemed to live much to himself in Columbus, as he always did, but I saw a great deal of him, for in the community of youth we had no want of things to talk about; we could always talk about ourselves when there was nothing else. He was in the prime of his vigorous manhood, with a fine red beard, and a close-cropped head of red hair, like Michelangelo, and a flattened nose like the Florentine's, so that I rejoiced in him as the ideal of a sculptor. I still think him, for certain Greek qualities, the greatest of American sculptors; his "Indian Hunter" in Central Park must bear witness of our historic difference from other peoples as long as bronze shall last, and as no other sculpture can. But the "Kenton" was never to be eternized in bronze or marble for that niche in the rotunda of the capital where Ward may have imagined it finding itself. The cloud thickened over us, and burst at last in the shot fired on Fort Sumter; the legislature appropriated a million dollars as the contribution of the state to the expenses of the war, and Ward's hopes vanished as utterly as if the bolt had smitten his plaster model into dust.

Before Ward, almost, indeed, with my first coming to Columbus, there had been another sculptor whom I was greatly interested to know. This was Thomas D. Jones, who had returned to Ohio from an attempt upon the jealous East, where he had suffered that want of appreciation which was apt, in a prevalent superstition of the West, to attend any æsthetic endeavor from our section. He frankly stood for the West, though I believe he was a Welshman by birth; but in spite of his pose he was a sculptor of real talent. He modeled a bust of Chase, admirable as a likeness, and of a very dignified simplicity. I do not know whether it was ever put in marble, but it was put in plaster very promptly and sold in many such replicas. The sculptor liked to be seen modeling it, and I can see him yet, stepping back a little from his work, and then advancing upon it with a sensitive twitching of his mustache and a black censorious frown. The Governor must have posed in the pleasant room which Jones had in the Neil House where he lived, how I do not know, for he was threadbare poor; but in those days many good things seemed without price to the debtor class; and very likely the management liked to have him there, where his work attracted people. One day while I was in the room the Governor came in and, not long after, a lady who appeared instinctively to time her arrival when it could be most largely impressive. As she was staying in the hotel, she wore nothing on her dewily disheveled hair, as it insists upon characterizing itself in the retrospect, and she had the effect of moving about on a stage. She had, in fact, just come up on some theatrical wave from her native Tennessee, and she had already sent her album of favorable notices to the *Journal* office with the appeal inscribed in a massive histrionic hand, "Anything but your silence, gentlemen!" She played a short engagement in Columbus, and then departed for the East and for the far grander capitals of the Old World, where she became universally famous as Ada Isaacs Menken, and finally by a stroke of her fearless imagination figured in print as the bride of the pugilist Heenan, then winning us the laurels of the ring away from English rivalry. I cannot recall, with all my passion for the theater, that I saw her on any stage but that which for a moment she made of the sculptor's room

Jones had been a friend from much earlier days, almost my earliest days in Columbus; it was he who took me to that German house, where I could scarcely gasp for the high excitement of finding myself with a lady who had known Heinrich Heine and could talk of him as if he were a human being. I had not become a hopeless drunkard from drinking the glass of eggnog which she gave me while she talked familiarly of him, and when after several years Jones took me to her house again she had the *savoir faire* quite to ignore the interval of neglect which I had

217

suffered to elapse, and gave me a glass of eggnog again. It must have been in 1859 that Jones vanished from my life, but I must not let him take with him a friend whose thoughtfulness at an important moment I still feel.

This was a man who afterward became known as the author of two curious books, entitled *Library Notes,* made up somewhat in the discursive fashion of Montaigne's essays, out of readings from his favorite authors. There was nothing original in them except the taste which guided their selection, but they distinctly gave the sort of pleasure he had in compiling them, and their readers will recall with affection the name of A. P. Russell. He was the Ohio Secretary of State when I knew him first, and he knew me as the stripling who was writing in his nonage the legislative letters of the Cincinnati *Gazette;* and he alone remembered me distinctly enough to commend me for a place on the staff of the *State Journal* when Mr. Cooke took control of it. After the war he spent several years in some financial service of the state in New York, vividly interested in the greatness of a city where, as he was fond of saying, a cannon-shot could be heard by eight hundred thousand people; six million people could hear it now if anything could make itself heard above the multitudinous noises that have multiplied themselves since. When his term of office ended he returned to Ohio, where he shunned cities great and small, and retired to the pleasant town where he was born, like an Italian to his *patria,* and there ended his peaceful, useful days. It was my good fortune in almost the last of these days to write and tell him of my unforgotten gratitude for that essential kindness he had done me so long before, and to have a letter back from him, the more touching because another's hand had written it; for Russell had become blind.

Probably he had tried to help Ward in his hope, which

was hardly a scheme, for that appropriation from the legislature for his "Simon Kenton." They always remained friends, and during Russell's stay in New York he probably saw more of Ward, so often sequestered with the horses for his equestrian groups, than most of his other friends. I who lived quarter of a century in the same city with him saw him seldom by that fault of social indolence, rather than indifference, which was always mine, and which grows upon one with the years. Once I went to dine with him in the little room off his great, yawning, equine studio, and to have him tell me of his life for use in a book of "Ohio Stories" I was writing; then some swift years afterward I heard casually from another friend that Ward was sick. "Would he be out soon?" I asked. "I don't think he'll be out at all," I was answered, and I went the next day to see him. He was lying with his fine head on the pillow still like such a head of Michelangelo as the Florentine might have modeled of himself, and he smiled and held out his hand, and had me sit down. We talked long of old times, of old friends and enemies (but not really enemies), and it was sweet to be with him so. He seemed so very like himself that it was hard to think him in danger, but he reminded us who were there that he was seventy-nine years old, and when we spoke about his getting well and soon being out again he smiled in the wisdom which the dying have from the world they are so near, and, tenderly patient of us, expressed his doubt. In a few days, before I could go again, I heard that he was dead.

XI

But in that winter of 1859-60, after Lincoln had been elected, Ward was still hopeful of an order from the state for his "Simon Kenton," and I was hopeful of the poetic pre-eminence which I am still foregoing. I used such scraps of time as I could filch from the busy days and nights and gave them to the verse which now seemed to come back from editors oftener than it once did. This hurt, but it did not kill, and I kept on at verse for years in the delusion that it was my calling and that I could make it my living. It was not until four or five years later that a more practical muse persuaded me my work belonged to her, and in the measureless leisure of my Venetian consulate I began to do the various things in prose which I have mostly been doing ever since, for fifty years past. Till then I had no real leisure, but was yet far from the days when anything less than a day seems too small a space to attempt anything in. That is the mood of age and of middle age, but youth seizes any handful of minutes and devotes them to some beginning or ending. It had been my habit ever since I took up journalism to use part of the hour I had for midday dinner in writing literature, and such hours of the night as were left me after my many calls or parties; and now I did not change, even under the stress of the tragical events crowding upon us all.

I phrase it so, but really I felt no stress, and I do not believe others felt it so much as the reader might think. As I look back upon it the whole state of affairs seems incredible, and to a generation remote from it must seem impossible. We had an entire section of the Republic openly seeking its dismemberment, and a government which permitted and even abetted the seizure of national property by its enemies and the devotion of its resources to its own destruction. With the worst coming, relentlessly, rapidly, audibly, visibly, no one apparently thought the worst would come; there had been so many threats of disunion before, and the measures now taken to effect it seemed only a more dramatic sort of threats. People's minds were confused by the facts which they could not accept as portents, and the North remained practically passive, while the South was passionately active; and yet not the whole South, for as yet Secession was not a condition, but merely a principle. There was a doubt with some in the North itself whether the right of disunion was not implied in the very act of union; there had long been a devoted minority who felt that disunion without slavery was better than union with slavery; and on both sides there arose sentimental cries, entreaties from the South that the North would yield its points of right and conscience, appeals from the North that the South would not secede until the nation had time to decide what it would do. The North would not allow itself to consider seriously of coercing the seceding states; and there was a party willing to bid them, with unavailing tears, "Erring sisters, go in peace," as if the seceding states, being thus delicately entreated, could not have the heart to go, even in peace. There were hysterical conferences of statesmen in and out of office to arrange for mutual concessions which were to be all on the part of the Union, or if not that then to order its decent obsequies.

I cannot make out that our chief had any settled policy for the conduct of our paper; nobody had a settled policy concerning public affairs. If his subordinates had any settled policy, it was to get what fun they could out of the sentimentalists, and if they had any fixed belief it was that if we had a war peace must be made on the basis of disunion when the war was over. In our wisdom we doubted if the sections could ever live together in a union which they had fought for and against. But we did not say this in print, though as matters grew more hopeless Price one day seized the occasion of declaring that the Constitution was a rope of sand. I do not remember what occasion he had for saying this, but it brought our chief actively back to the censorship; Price's position was somehow explained away, and we went on as much as before, much as everybody else went on. I will not, in the confession of our youthful rashness, pretend that there were any journalists who seemed then or seem wiser now or acted with greater forecast; and I am sure that we always spoke from our consciences, with a settled conviction that the South was wrong. We must have given rather an ironical welcome to a sufficently muddled overture of the Tennessee legislature which during the winter sent a deputation of its members to visit our own Houses and confer with them as to what might be done. The incident now has it pathos, there was so much that was well meant in the attempt to mend our bad business with kind words and warm feelings, though then I was sensible only of its absurdity. I did not hear any of the speeches, but I remember seeing the Tennessee statesmen about the Capitol for the different conferences held there and noting that some of them spoke with a negroid intonation and not with that Ohio accent which I believed the best in the English-speaking world. No doubt they parted with our own legislators affectionately, and returned home supported by the hope that they had really done something in a case where there was nothing to be done.

Their endeavor was respectable, but there was no change in the civic conditions except from bad to worse. In the social conditions, or the society conditions, everything was for the better, if indeed these could be bettered in Columbus. Of all the winters this was the gayest; society was kind again, after I had paid the penalty it exacted for my neglect, and I began to forget my purpose of living in air more absolutely literary. Again I began going the rounds of the friendly houses, but now, as if to win my fancy more utterly, there began to be a series of dances in a place and on conditions the most alluring. For a while after the functions of the medical school were suspended in the College where I had lodged, the large ward where the lectures were once given was turned into a gymnasium and fitted up with the usual gymnastic apparatus. I do not recall whether this was taken away or not, or was merely looped up and put aside for our dances, and I do not know how we came into possession of the place; in the retrospect, such things happen in youth much as things happen in childhood, without apparent human agency; but at any rate we had this noble circus for our dances. There must have been some means of joining them, but it is now gone from me, and I know only that they were given under the fully sufficing chaperonage of a sole matron. There were two negro fiddlers, and the place was lighted by candles fixed along the wall; but memory does not serve me as to any sort of supper; probably there was none, except such as the young men, after they had seen the young ladies to their homes, went up-town to make on the oysters of Ambos.

It is strange that within the time so dense with incident for us there should have been so few incidents now separately tangible, but there is one that vividly distinguishes itself from the others. In that past I counted any experience precious that seemed to parallel the things of fact with the things of fiction. Afterward, but long afterward, I learned to praise, perhaps too arrogantly praise, the things of fiction as they paralleled the things of fact, but as yet it was not so. I suppose the young are always like us as we of the College dances were then, but romance can rarely offer itself to youth of any time in the sort of reality which one night enriched us amid our mirth with a wild thrill of dismay at the shriek in a girl's voice of "Dead?" There was an instant halt in the music, and then a rush to the place where the cry had risen. Somebody had fainted, and when the fact could be verified, it was found that one of the blithest of our company had been struck down with word from home that her sister had fallen dead of heart failure. Then when we began to falter away from the poor child's withdrawal, suddenly another tumult stayed us; a young father, who had left his first-born with its mother in their rooms above while he came down for some turns in the waltz, could not believe that it was not his child that was dead, and he had to be pulled and pushed up-stairs into sight and sound of the little one roused from its sleep to convince him, before he could trust the truth.

Here was mingling of the tragic and the comic to the full admired effect of Shakespearian drama, but the mere circumstance of these esthetic satisfactions would have been emotional wealth enough; and when I got home on such a night to my slumbering room-mate Price I could give myself in glad abandon to the control of the poet whose psychic I then oftenest was, with some such result as I found in a tattered manuscript the other day. I think the poet could hardly have resented my masking in his wonted self-mocking, though I am afraid that he would have shrunk from the antic German which I put on to the beat of his music.

> "To-night there is dancing and fiddling
> In the high windowed hall
> Lighted with dim corpse-candles
> In bottles against the wall.
>
> "And the people talk of the weather,
> And say they think it will snow;
> And, without, the wind in the gables
> Moans wearily and low.

224

"'*Sa! Sa!*'—the dance of the Phantoms!
  The dim corpse-candles flare;
On the whirl of the flying spectres
  The shuddering windows stare.

"'Oh, play us the silent Ghost-Waltz,
  Thou fiddling blackamoor!'
He hears the ghostly summons,
  He sees the ghosts on the floor.

"He plays the silent Ghost-Waltz
  And through the death-mute hall
The voiceless echoes answer,
  In time the ghost-feet fall.

"Und immer und immer schneller,
  Und wild wie der Winterwind
Die beide College Gespenster
  Sie walzen sinnengeschwind.

"They waltz to the open doorway,
  They waltz up the winding stair:
'Oh, gentle ghosts we are sneezing,
  We are taking cold in the air.'"

XII

Very likely those dances lasted through the winter, but
I cannot be sure; I can only be sure that they summed up
the raptures of the time, which was the most memorable
of my whole life; for now I met her who was to be my
wife. We were married the next year, and she became
with her unerring artistic taste and conscience my constant impulse toward reality and sincerity in my work.
She was the first to blame and the first to praise, as she
was the first to read what I wrote. Forty-seven years we
were together here, and then she died. But in that gay-

est time when we met it did not seem as if there could ever be an end of time for us, or any time less radiant. Though the country was drawing nearer and nearer the abyss where it plunged so soon, few thought it would make the plunge; many believed that when it would it could draw back from it, but doubtless that was never possible; there is a doom for nations as there is for men, and looking back upon our history I cannot see how we could have escaped. The slaveholders in the old Union were a few hundred thousand against many millions, but a force in them beyond their own control incessantly sought to control the non-slaveholding majority. They did not brook question of their will from others; they brooked no self-question of it; however little they seemed at moments to demand, they never demanded less than that conscience itself should come to their help in making their evil our good. Having said that black was white, that wrong was right, they were vitally bound to compel the practical consent of humanity. If was what it had been aforetime and must be to aftertime; Lincoln did not deny them in terms different from Franklin's, but the case had gone farther. The hour had come when they would not be denied at all; slavery could never keep its promises; it could hardly stay even to threaten. Long before there had been dreams of ending it by buying the slaves, but the owners would not have sold their slaves, and now, though the war against slavery tried to believe itself a war for the Union, when it came to full consciousness it knew itself a war for freedom; such freedom, lame and halt, as we have been able to keep for the negroes; a war for democracy, such democracy as we shall not have for ourselves until we have an economic democracy.

The prevision of the young writers on the *State Journal* was of no such reach as this retrospect. The best that

could be said of them was that so far as they knew the
right, they served it, and it is no bad thing to say of them
that they met insolence with ridicule and hypocrisy with
contempt. Still, as always before in those columns,
they got their fun out of the opportunities which the
situation offered, and they did not believe the worst was
coming; that would excuse their levity, and it availed
as much as gravity. I do not remember that we took
counsel with any one as to what we said or that we
consulted much with each other. We did not think
that the Union would be dissolved, but if it should be
we did not think that its dissolution was the worst thing
that could happen; and this was the mind of vastly
more at that day than most at this day will believe;
some of those who were of that mind then may not like
to own it now. People have the habit of saying that
only those who have lived through a certain period can
realize it, but I doubt if even they can realize it. A
civic agitation is like a battle; it covers a surface so large
that only a part of it can be seen by any one spectator at
any one moment. The fact seems to be that the most
of human motives and actions must always remain obscure;
history may do its best to record and reveal them, but
it will strive in vain to give us a living sense of them,
because no one ever had a living sense of them in their
entirety.

At the period which I am trying to tell of the hours
passed and the days and weeks and months, bringing
us forever nearer the catastrophe; but I could not truthfully say that their passing changed the general mood.
The College group which I used to consort with had
changed, and it was no longer so much to my liking;
it had dwindled, and for me it chiefly remained in the
companionship of one friend, whom I walked and talked
with when I was not walking and talking with Price.

This was that protested and rejected Clive Newcome, of ours, who in real life was James M. Comly, law student then, and then soldier, and then journalist. Of all the friends in whose contrast I have been trying to find myself, he was temperamentally the most unlike me, but a common literary bent inclined us to each other. In his room there was not only euchre for those who could not bear to waste in idleness the half-hours before dinner or supper, but there were the latest fashions in such periodicals as the *Cornhill Magazine*, then so brand new, and the *Saturday Review*, equally new, with the great Thackeray stooping from his Jovian height in the monthly to blunt against the weekly, with its social and critical offensives, such bolts as calling it the *Superfine Review*. Comly was of much the same taste as myself in authors, but not so impassioned; he was not so multifarious a reader and not so inclusive of the poets, and in obedience to his legalist instincts he was of more conservative feeling in politics. We had never a moment of misgiving for each other, yet I had one bad moment over an *Atlantic* poem of mine fabling the author as a bird singing in a tree, and flatteringly but unintelligently listened to by the cattle beneath which the title of the piece typified as "The Poet's Friends." The conceit had overtempted me, but when I had realized it in print, with no sense meantime of its possible relevance, I felt the need of bringing myself to book with the friend I valued most, and urging how innocently literary, how most merely and entirely dramatic the situation was. I think my anxiety amused him, as it very well might, but I still draw a long breath of relief when I remember how perfectly he understood.

Our association was mostly in the walks we took in the winter twilights and the summer moonlights, walks long enough in the far-stretching Columbus streets to have encompassed the globe; but our talks were not nearly so long as the walks, walks in which there were reaches of reticence, when apparently it was enough for us to be walking together. Yet we must often have talked about the books we were reading, that is to say the novels, though seldom about public events, which is the stranger, or the less strange, because as a student of law he was of course a potential politician, and I was writing politics every day.

He was the last but one of the friends whom my youth was so rich in, for no reason more, perhaps, than that we were young together, though they were all older than I, and Comly was five or six years my senior. When I knew him first, with his tall, straight figure, his features of Greek fineness, his blue eyes, and his moustache thin and ashen blond, he was of a distinction fitting the soldier he became when the Civil War began, and he fought through the four years' struggle with such gallantry and efficiency that he came out of it with the rank of brigadier-general. He had broken with the law amid arms, and in due time he succeeded to the control of our newspaper where he kept on terms of his own the tradition of Reed, which Price and I had continued in our fashion, and made the paper an increasing power. But he had never been the vigorous strength he looked, and after certain years of overwork he accepted the appointment of minister to Hawaii. The rest and the mild climate renewed his health, and he came back to journalism under different conditions of place. But the strain was the same; he gave way under it again, and died a few years later.

XIII

I cannot make out why, having the friends and incentives I had in Columbus, I should have wished to go away, but more and more I did wish that. There was no reason for it except my belief that my work would be less acceptable if I remained in the West; that I should get on faster if I wrote in New York than if I wrote in Columbus. Somehow I fancied there would be more intellectual atmosphere for me in the great city, but I do not believe this now, and I cannot see how I could anywhere have had more intelligent sympathy. When I came home from Venice in 1865, and was looking about for some means of livelihood, I found that Lowell had a fancy for my returning to the West, and living my literary life in my own air if not on my own ground. He apparently thought the experiment would be interesting; and if I were again twenty-eight I should like to try it. I would indeed have been glad then of any humble place on a newspaper in the West; but the East more hospitably entreated me, and after a flattering venture in New York journalism I was asked to the place in Boston which of all others in the world was that I could most have desired.

In those Columbus days I was vaguely aware that if I went farther from home I should be homesick, for where I was, in that happy environment, I was sometimes almost intolerably homesick. From my letters home I find that I was vividly concerned in the affairs of those I had left there, striving and saving to pay for the printing-office and the house with so little help from me. I was still sometimes haunted by the hypochondria which had once blackened my waking hours with despair; I dare say I was always overworking, and bringing my fear upon me out of the exhaustion of my nerves. Perhaps I am confiding too much when I speak of this most real, most unreal misery, but if the confession of it will help any who suffer, especially in the solitude of youth which inexperience makes a prison-house, I shall not be ashamed of what some may impute to me for weakness. If one knows

there is some one else who is suffering in his kind, then
one can bear it better; and in this way, perhaps, men
are enabled to go to their death in battle, where they
die with thousands of others; in the multitudinous doom
of the Last Day its judgments may not be so dreadful to the single culprit. Like every one who lives, I
was a congeries of contradictions, willing to play with the
fancies that came to me, but afraid of them if they stayed
too late. Yet I did not lose much sleep from them; it is
after youth is gone that we begin to lose sleep from care;
while our years are few we indeed rise up with care, but
it does not wake night-long with us, as it does when our
years are more.

I had a most cheerful companion in my colleague,
Price, who so loved to laugh and to make laugh. If he
never made the calls or went to the parties to which
I tempted him, apparently he found our own society
sufficient, and, in fact, I could not wish for anything
better myself than when, the day's work and the night's
pleasure ended for me, we sat together in the editorial-
room, where our chief seldom molested us, and waited
for the last telegraphic despatches before sending the
paper to press. Sometimes we had the company of
officials from the State House who came over to while
away the hours, more haggard for them than for us, with
the stories they told while we listened. They were often
such stories as Lincoln liked, no doubt for the humorous
human nature and racy character in them. Very likely
he found a relief in them from the tragedy overhanging
us all, but not molesting our young souls with the portents which the sad-eyed man of duty and of doom was
aware of, or perhaps not yet aware of.

The strangest impression that the time has left with
me is a sense of the patient ignorance which seemed to
involve the whole North. Doubtless the South, or the

more positive part of it, knew what it was about; but the North could only theorize and conjecture and wait while those who were in keeping of the nation were seeking its life. In the glare of the events that followed volcanically enough, it seems as if the North must have been of the single mind which it became when the shot fired on Fort Sumter woke it at last to the fact that the country was really in peril. But throughout the long suspense after Lincoln's election till his inauguration there was no settled purpose in the North to save the Union, much less to fight for it. People ate and slept for the most part tranquilly throughout; they married and gave in marriage; they followed their dead to the grave with no thought that the dead were well out of the world; they bought and sold, and got gain; what seemed the end could not be the end, because it had never come before.

After the war actually began we could not feel that it had begun; we had the evidence of our senses, but not of our experiences; in most things it was too like peace to be really war. Neither of the great sections believed in the other, but the South, which was solidified by the slaveholding caste, had the advantage of believing in itself, and the North did not believe in itself till the fighting began. Then it believed too much and despised the enemy at its throat. Among the grotesque instances of our self-confidence I recall the consoling assurance of an old friend, a chief citizen and wise in his science, who said, as the hostile forces were approaching each other in Virginia, "Oh, they will run," and he meant the Southerners, as he lifted his fine head and blew a whiff from his pipe into the air. "As soon as they see we are in earnest they will run," but it was not from us that they ran; and the North was startled from its fallacy that sixty days would see the end of the rebellion, whose end no prophet had now the courage to forecast. We of the

232

Ohio capital were a very political community, the most
political in the whole state, in virtue of our being the
capital, but none of the rumors of war had distracted us
from our pleasures or affairs, at least so far as the eyes of
youth could see. With our faith in the good ending, as if
our national story were a tale that must end well, with
whatever suspenses, or thrilling episodes, we had put the
day's anxieties by and hopefully waited for the morrow's
consolations. But when the fateful shot was fired at
Fort Sumter, it was as if the echo had not died away when
a great public meeting was held in response to the President's call for volunteers, and the volunteering began
with an effect of simultaneity which the foreshortening
of past events always puts on to the retrospective eye.
It seemed as if it were only the night before that we had
listened to the young Patti, now so old, singing her
sweetest in that hall where the warlike appeals rang out,
with words smiting like blows in that "Anvil Chorus"
which between her songs had thrilled us with the belief
that we were listening to the noblest as well as the newest
music in the world.

I have sometimes thought that I would write a novel,
with its scene in our capital at that supreme moment
when the volunteering began, but I shall never do it,
and without the mask of fiction one cannot give the living
complexion of events. Instantly the town was inundated
from all the towns of the state and from the farms between
as with a tidal wave of youth; for most of those who
flooded our streets were boys of eighteen and twenty,
and they came in the wild hilarity of their young vision,
singing by day and by night, one sad inconsequent song,
that filled the whole air, and that fills my sense yet as I
think of them:

"Oh, nebber mind the weather, but git ober double trouble,
  For we're bound for the happy land of Canaan."

YEARS OF MY YOUTH

They wore red shirts, as if the color of the Garibaldian war for Union in Italy had flashed itself across the sea to be the hue of our own war for Union. With interlinked arms they ranged up and down, and pushed the willing citizens from the pavement, and shouted the day and shouted the night away, with no care but the fear that in the outpour of their death-daring they might not be gathered into the ranks filling up the quota of regiments assigned to Ohio. The time had a sublimity which no other time can know, unless some proportionate event shall again cause the nation to stand up as one man, and the spectacle had a mystery and an awe which I cannot hope to impart. I knew that these boys, bursting from their fields and shops as for a holiday, were just such boys as I had always known, and if I looked at any one of them as they went swaggering and singing up and down I recognized him for what they were, but in their straggling ranks, with their young faces flushed the red of the blouses and their young eyes flaming, I beheld them transfigured. I do not pretend that they were of the make of armies such as I had seen pictured marching in serried ranks to battle, and falling in bloody windrows on the smoke-rolled plain. All that belonged to

" Old, unhappy, far-off days,"

and not to the morrows in which I dwelt. But possibly if I had written that forever-to-be-unwritten novel I might have plucked out the heart of the moment and laid it throbbing before the reader; and yet I might rather have been satisfied with the more subjective riddle of one who looked on, and baffled himself with question of the event.

Only two or three of the friends who had formed our College group went to the war; of these my friend Comly, had been one of the earliest, and when I found him officer of the day at the first camp of the volunteers, he gave me what time he could, but he was helplessly preoccupied, and the whole world I had known was estranged. One morning I met another friend, coming down the State House steps and smiling radiantly; he also was a law student, and he had just been made adjutant of a newly accepted regiment. Almost immediately afterward he was changed to the line, and at the end of the war, after winning its last important battle, John G. Mitchell came out with the rank of brigadier-general, to which the brevet of major-general could scarcely add distinction. By the chances which play with our relations in life I had not known him so well as some others. He was not of the College group; but after the war we came familiarly together in the friendship of the cousins who had become our wives. In that after-time he once held me rapt with the stories of his soldier life, promising, or half promising, to put them down for print, but never doing it, so that now they are lost to that record of personal experience of battle which forms so vital a part of our history. No stories of that life which I have read have seemed to me so frank, so full, so real, as those he told.

Our first camp was in our pretty Goodale Park, where I used to walk and talk with the sculptor Ward, and try the athletic feats in which he easily beat me. Now the pine sheds covered the long tables, spread with coffee and pork and beans, and the rude bunks filled with straw, and here and there a boy volunteer frowzily drowsing in them. It was one of the many shapeless beginnings which were to end in the review of the hundred thousands of seasoned soldiers marching to their mustering out in Washington after four years of fire and blood. No one could imagine that any of these boys were to pass through that abyss, or that they would not come safely out. Even after the cruel disillusion of Manassas the superstition

235

of quick work remained with the North, and the three years' quota of Ohio was filled almost as jubilantly as the three months', but not quite so jubilantly. Sons and brothers came with tears to replace fathers and brothers who had not returned from Manassas, and there was a funeral undertone in the shrilling of the fifes and the throbbing of the drums which was not so before. Life is like Hamlet and will oftentimes "put an antic disposition on," which I have never been one to refuse recognition, and now I must, with whatever effect from it, own a bit of its mockery. One of our reporters was a father whose son had been among the first to go, and word came that the boy had been killed at Manassas. I liked the father as I had liked the son, and the old man's grief moved me to such poor offer of consolation as verse could make. He was deeply touched, but the next day another word came that the boy was alive and well, and I could not leave my elegiacs with his father, who was apparently reluctant to renounce the glory of them, although so glad. But he gave them back, and I depersonalized them by removing the name of the young soldier, and finally printed them in the volume of poems which two or three people still buy every year.

XIV

It was a question now whether I could get the appointment of a consulate which I had already applied for, quite as much, I believe, upon the incentive of my fellow-citizens as from a very natural desire of my own. It seemed to be the universal feeling, after the election of Lincoln, that I who had written his life ought to have a consulate, as had happened with Hawthorne, who had written the life of Franklin Pierce. It was thought a very fitting thing, and my fellow-citizens appeared willing I should

have any consulate, but I, with constitutional unhopeful-
ness, had fixed my mind upon that of Munich, as in the
way to further study of the German language and literature, and this was the post I asked for in an application
signed by every prominent Republican in the capital, from
the Governor down. The Governor was now William
Dennison, who afterward became Postmaster-General,
and who had always been my friend, rather in the measure
of his charming good will than my merit, from my first
coming to Columbus; Chase had already entered Lincoln's
Cabinet as Secretary of the Treasury. But in spite
of this backing the President, with other things on his
mind, did not respond in any way until some months
had dragged by, when one day I received without warn-
ing an official envelope addressed to me as "Consul at
Rome, now at Columbus, Ohio." Rome was not exactly
Munich, and the local language and literature were not
German, but I could not have expected the State Department to take cognizance of a tacit ideal of mine, and the
consulate was at any rate a consulate, which perhaps
most of my friends supposed was what I wanted. It was
welcome enough, for I was again to be dropped from the
high horse which I had been riding for nearly a year past;
one of those changes in the *State Journal* which Greeley,
in his unsolicited lecture, had imputed to it for unworthi-
ness was at hand, and the gentleman who was buying a
controlling share in it might or might not wish to write
the editorials himself. At any rate the Roman consulship
was not to be declined without inquiry, but as there was
no salary, and the consul was supposed to live upon the
fees taken, I tried to find out how much the fees might
annually come to. Meanwhile I was advised by prudence
to accept the appointment provisionally; it would be
easy to resign it if I could not afford to keep it; and I
waited to see what the new proprietor meant to do.

Apparently he meant to be editor as well as proprietor, and Price and I must go, which we made ready to do as soon as the new proprietor came into his own. Three or four times in my life I have suffered some such fate as I suffered then; but I never lost a place except through the misfortune of those who gave it me; then with whatever heart I could I accepted the inevitable. At the worst, I was yet "Consul at Rome now at Columbus," and I had my determination to work. I was never hopeful, I was never courageous, but somehow I was dogged. I had no overweening belief in myself, and yet I thought, at the bottom of my soul, that I had in me the make of the thing I was bent on doing, the thing literature, the greatest thing in the world.

When our new proprietor arrived Price and I disabled his superiority, probably on no very sufficient grounds, but he had the advantage in not wanting our help, and I decided to go to Washington and look personally into the facts of the Roman consulship. As perhaps some readers of this may know, it ultimately turned into the Venetian consulship, but by just what friendly magic, has been told with sufficient detail in a chapter of *Literary Friends and Acquaintance* and need not be rehearsed here. As for Price, he had nothing at all before him, but he was by no means uncheerful. We had certainly had a joyous though parlous year together; our jokes could not have been numbered in a season when the only excuse for joking was that it might as well be that as weeping, though probably we had our serious times, especially when we foreboded a fresh dismay in our chief at some escapade in derision or denunciation of the well-meaning patriots' efforts to hold the Union together with mucilage.

But the time came when all this tragical mirth was to end. We found that we did not dislike the new owner, and he liked us well enough, but he was eager to try his hand at our work, and some time early in August we quitted the familiar place. If there was any form of adieu with our gentle chief I do not remember it, and in fact my mind holds no detail of our parting except the last hour of it, when we found ourselves together at midnight in the long, gloomy barn then known as the Little Miami Depot, where we were to take our separate ways in the dark which hid us from each other forever. We walked up and down a long time, talking, talking, talking, laughing, promising each other to be faithful in letters, and wearing our souls out in the nothings which people say at such times with the vain endeavor to hold themselves together against the fate which is to sunder them in the voluntary death of parting. We heard the whistle of an approaching train, we shook hands, we said goodby, and then in a long wait repeated the nothings again and again. But my train on the Central Ohio was already there; and as Price obeyed the call to board his train for Cleveland, I mounted mine for Washington, and we never saw each other again. It is long since he died, and I who still survive him after fifty years offer his memory this vow of abiding affection. If we somewhere should somewhen meet, perhaps it will be with a fond smile for the time we were young and so glad together, with so little reason.

THE END